A NIGHT AT THE OPERA

THE MGM LIBRARY OF FILM SCRIPTS

Ninotchka

North by Northwest

Adam's Rib

Singin' in the Rain

A Day at the Races

A Night at the Opera

A Night at the Opera

Screenplay by George S. Kaufman and Morrie Ryskind

Story by James Kevin McGuinness

A VIKING FILM BOOK

NEW YORK / *The Viking Press*

Published in 1972 in a hardbound and paperbound edition by
The Viking Press, Inc.
625 Madison Avenue, New York, N.Y. 10022
Published simultaneously in Canada by
The Macmillan Company of Canada Limited
SBN 670-51129-3 (hardbound)
    670-01948-8 (paperbound)
Library of Congress catalog card number: 75-178818
Printed in U.S.A.

ACKNOWLEDGMENT
Robbins Music Corporation: "Alone." Lyrics: Arthur Freed;
Music: Nacio Herb Brown.
Copyright 1935, Renewed 1962 Robbins Music Corporation.
"Cosi Cosa." Lyrics: Ned Washington; Music: Bronislaw Kaper, Walter Jurmann.
Copyright 1935, Renewed 1962 Robbins Music Corporation.
Used by permission.

128028

CREDITS

Production	Metro-Goldwyn-Mayer
Produced by	Irving Thalberg
Directed by	Sam Wood
Screenplay by	George S. Kaufman and Morrie Ryskind
Story by	James Kevin McGuinness
Musical Score by	Herbert Stothart
Song: "Alone"	
Music	Nacio Herb Brown
Lyrics	Arthur Freed
Song: "Cosi-Cosa"	
Music	Bronislau Kaper and Walter Jurmann
Lyrics	Ned Washington
Dances by	Chester Hale
Director of Photography	Merritt B. Gerstad, A.S.C.
Art Director	Cedric Gibbons
Associates	Ben Carre and Edwin S. Willis
Film Editor	William Levanway
Recording Director	Douglas Shearer
Wardrobe	Dolly Tree
Time	96 minutes
Released	1935

CAST

OTIS B. DRIFTWOOD	Groucho Marx
FIORELLO	Chico Marx
TOMASSO	Harpo Marx
ROSA CASTALDI	Kitty Carlisle
RICARDO BARONI	Allan Jones
RUDOLFO LASSPARRI	Walter Woolf King
HERMAN GOTTLIEB	Sig Rumann

v

MRS. CLAYPOOL	Margaret Dumont
CAPTAIN	Edward Keane
DETECTIVE HENDERSON	Robert Emmett O'Connor
STEWARD	Gino Corrado
MAYOR	Purnell Pratt
ENGINEER	Frank Yaconelli
ENGINEER'S ASSISTANT/ PEASANT	Billy Gilbert
EXTRA ON SHIP AND AT DOCK	Sam Marx
POLICE CAPTAIN	Claude Peyton
DANCERS	Rita and Rubin
RUIZ	Luther Hoobyar
COUNT DI LUNA	Rodolfo Hoyos
AZUCENA (GYPSY WOMAN)	Olga Dane
FERRANDO	James J. Wolf
MAID	Ines Palange
STAGE MANAGER	Jonathan Hale
ELEVATOR MAN	Otto Fries
CAPTAIN OF POLICE	William Gould
AVIATORS	Leo White, Jay Eaton, Rolfe Sedan
COMMITTEE	Wilbur Mack, George Irving
POLICEMAN	George Guhl
SIGN PAINTER	Harry Tyler
COMMITTEE	Phillips Smalley, Selmer Jackson
IMMIGRATION INSPECTOR	Alan Bridge
DOORMAN	Harry Allen
LOUISA	Lorraine Bridges

NOTE

Because the final film differs so much from the script, this volume includes both the original script and the dialogue and action in the film itself.

THE ORIGINAL SCRIPT

The head of Leo, the Lion, appears on the screen and roars three times. Then the lion's head fades and CHICO's *appears. At the same time the Latin inscription,* ARS GRATIA ARTIS, *changes into* MARX GRATIA MARXES. CHICO *imitates the lion opening his mouth. As his mouth opens, the lion's roar is dubbed in.* CHICO's *head is replaced by* GROUCHO's *and the same imitation of the mouth opening is done, with the lion's roar dubbed in again. Now* GROUCHO's *head is replaced by* HARPO's. *He opens his mouth twice and tries to roar, but no sound is heard. So* HARPO *reaches out of the scroll and comes up with his bulbous automobile horn. Once more opening his mouth, he holds the horn beside it and toots twice at the audience. He grins in triumph. His face* FADES OUT *and the regular main titles* FADE IN.

Behind the main and credit titles is heard the orchestral music of the principal aria of Pagliacci.

Store Window, Milan Street—Night
The CAMERA FRAMES *on a cardboard sign in a somewhat dirty store window, which is filled with vegetables, Italian groceries, etc. The placard reads:*

ITALIAN OPERA COMPANY
MILAN
Rudolfo Lassparri
in
Pagliacci
LAST NIGHT OF SEASON

3

Street Scene, Milan—Night

This is a street in one of the humbler sections of Milan. The music continues under this and succeeding scenes. A STREET CLEANER *is seen, brushing in the exact tempo of the music, toward the curbing. He is humming, or singing a snatch from the opera, the same bars that the orchestra is playing. As he reaches the curb, he throws his broom down, spreading his arms open in a happy gesture as he hits a high note.*

Then, triumphantly, he produces a ticket for the highest gallery of the opera and flourishes it toward a fat, heavily mustached, elderly Italian SHOPKEEPER, *still singing.*

Shot Toward Doorway of Store

The STREET CLEANER *is in the foreground, now taking off his heavy leather apron. The stout* SHOPKEEPER—*probably a vegetable and grocery store owner—is shrugging into his coat. As he puts it on, standing in the doorway, he takes up the song of the* STREET CLEANER, *doing it in deep bass. At the same time, he produces about fifteen tickets and spreads them out, fanwise, to match the* STREET CLEANER's *triumph.*

Through the doorway of the shop comes a procession of about TWELVE CHILDREN—*ranging in age from a tot barely able to toddle, to a maiden of eighteen. Bringing up the rear, very much like a shepherdess after a flock, is the* MOTHER *of this brood. She, too, is a very generously proportioned dame. The whole troop starts down the street—the* STREET CLEANER *tossing his apron into the store as he passes. They are still singing snatches of the opera as they go.*

Another Street—in Front of Barracks

This is a very old and thick wall, with a heavy, somewhat rusted, wrought-iron gate. A SENTRY *is standing outside the gate. A dapper young* CAPTAIN OF THE BESAGLIERI, *in full dress, comes through the gate, singing a further snatch of the operatic air—continuing from the* SHOPKEEPER. *He jauntily*

4

acknowledges the SENTRY's *salute. Outside the gate a* STREET
VIOLINIST *is playing—shabbily dressed—synchronizing with
the orchestral music. Without stopping his jaunty song, the*
OFFICER *notices the* VIOLINIST, *and spins a coin through the
air at him.*

Street—Exclusive Residential District

*This might be in front of a hillside mansion. A very distin-
guished* OLD GENTLEMAN, *in formal dress with a sash across
his shirt front, is helping his gray-haired and pleasant-looking*
WIFE *into an Isotta Fraschini town car.*

*He is smiling and humming—although very gently—in con-
tinuation of the* OFFICER's *song. He steps into the car and the*
FOOTMAN *closes the door behind him. As the* FOOTMAN *walks
around to climb in beside the* CHAUFFEUR, *he continues the
music by whistling.*

Street—in Front of Cathedral

(NOTE: *It would be swell if we had a shot of the Cathedral
of Milan, against which this scene could be processed*)

An ARCHBISHOP—*a man with white hair and a benign
face—has just reached the bottom step of the cathedral. He is
accompanied by* TWO YOUNG PRIESTS, *who walk deferentially
about half a pace behind him. The* TWO YOUNG PRIESTS *are
humming, very softly. The* ARCHBISHOP *is smiling pleasantly,
almost ready to hum himself, but resisting it as somewhat
undignified. He responds in kindly fashion to the salutes of the
faithful passing by.*

Interior, Lobby—Hotel Italia, *the* ROOM CLERK's *desk. Leaning
against a pillar is a cardboard poster reading:*

ITALIAN OPERA COMPANY
Rudolfo Lassparri
in
Pagliacci

And across one corner of the poster a diagonal poster with FINAL PERFORMANCE OF THE SEASON *printed on it. . . . The* CLERK *is sorting the mail, humming to the operatic air as he does so. A* WOMAN *comes up to the desk.*

THE WOMAN: Room four thirty-eight, please.

The CLERK *hands her a key and her mail.*

A PORTER *comes into the scene, carrying luggage on a truck—and humming, of course. The* CAMERA FOLLOWS HIM *to a service elevator, where he dumps the trunk. As he does so, a* WAITER *comes into the scene, carrying a loaded tray. He picks up the music from the* PORTER; *for a moment they sing happily together. Then, with a smile, the* WAITER *proceeds on his way, the* CAMERA FOLLOWING.

The WAITER *enters the dining room. He passes a* GUEST *who is busily putting away spaghetti, still to the music. The* WAITER *stops just long enough to take a single note with him, then passes on to:*

Mrs. Claypool's Table

She is a young and handsome widow, is in evening clothes, and sitting alone. She looks at her wrist watch; her foot taps the floor impatiently; obviously she is in a mood . . . At the table behind her there sit a MAN *and a* GIRL. *The* GIRL, *a beautiful blond, faces* THE CAMERA; *the* MAN, *whose face we do not see, has his back to* MRS. CLAYPOOL. *A wine bottle is visible on their table.*

WAITER (*to* MRS. CLAYPOOL): The gentleman has not yet arrived.

MRS. CLAYPOOL (*furious*): No, he has not!

WAITER: But the dinner will be spoiled, Madame.

MRS. CLAYPOOL: What's the difference? It's too late to eat now! (*A* PAGE *is passing*) Boy! (*he comes to attention*) Will you page Mr. Driftwood, please? Mr. Otis B. Driftwood. (*She fairly bites off the name*)

THE PAGE (*going on his way*): Mr. Driftwood! Paging Mr. Driftwood! Mr. Driftwood!

The BLONDE *at the next table gives a little tinkly laugh. Her* COMPANION *joins in boisterously; tilting his chair back a little, he carelessly throws his cigar ashes over his shoulder. They drip down* MRS. CLAYPOOL's *alabaster back—there is a quick close-up of this bit—but* MRS. CLAYPOOL *remains blissfully unaware.*

Through all of this the voice of the PAGE *has never ceased—* "Paging Mr. Driftwood! Paging Mr. Driftwood!" *It now grows louder again; the* PAGE *is passing by.*

THE PAGE: Mr. Driftwood! Mr. Driftwood!

The CAMERA *now reveals the man at the adjoining table. It is, of course,* GROUCHO.

GROUCHO: Boy! *(The* PAGE *stops)* Will you do me a favor and stop yelling my name all over this restaurant? Do I go around yelling your name?

MRS. CLAYPOOL, *recognizing Groucho's voice, now turns on him in fury.*

MRS. CLAYPOOL: *Mr.* Driftwood!

GROUCHO *arising and moving toward the* PAGE, *says:*

GROUCHO: Say, is your voice changing, or is someone else paging me?

MRS. CLAYPOOL *(angrily)*: Mr. Driftwood—

GROUCHO *(turning)*: Why Mrs. Claypool! Halloo!

MRS. CLAYPOOL: Mr. Driftwood, you invited me to dine with you at seven o'clock! It is now eight o'clock, and no dinner!

GROUCHO: What do you mean, no dinner? I've just had one of the biggest meals I ever ate in my life, and no thanks to you, either.

MRS. CLAYPOOL: I have been sitting right here since seven o'clock.

GROUCHO: Yes, with your back to me. When I invite a woman to dinner, I expect her to look at my face. That's the price she has to pay. *(As the* WAITER *hands him the check)* Nine dollars and forty-three cents. This is an outrage. *(He hands the check to the other* GIRL*)* If I were you I wouldn't pay it. *(As he turns back to* MRS. CLAYPOOL*)* Now then, Mrs. Claypool, what are we going to have for dinner?

MRS. CLAYPOOL: But you've just had dinner.

GROUCHO: All right then, we'll have breakfast. *(To a passing WAITER)* Waiter! Have you any milk-fed chickens?

WAITER: Oh yes, sir.

GROUCHO: Well, squeeze the milk out of one and bring me a glass—

MRS. CLAYPOOL *(icily)*: Mr. Driftwood, three months ago you promised to put me into society. In all that time, you have done nothing but draw a very handsome salary.

GROUCHO *(indignantly)*: You think that's nothing, huh? How many men do you suppose are drawing a handsome salary nowadays? Why, you can count 'em on the fingers of one hand, my good woman.

MRS. CLAYPOOL: *I am not your good woman!*

GROUCHO: Don't say that, Mrs. Claypool. I don't care what your past has been—to me you are my good woman! Because I love you! There . . . I didn't mean to tell you, but you dragged it out of me. I love you!

MRS. CLAYPOOL: Oh, come now, Mr. Driftwood. It's a little hard to believe that, when I find you dining with another woman.

GROUCHO: That woman? Do you know why I sat down with her? Because she reminded me of you.

MRS. CLAYPOOL *(pleased)*: Really?

GROUCHO: Of course. That's why I'm here with *you*—because you remind me of you. Your eyes, your throat, your lips—everything reminds me of you. Except you. How do you account for that? *(He turns to the* CAMERA*)* If she figures that one out she's good.

MRS. CLAYPOOL: I think, Mr. Driftwood, that we had better keep everything on a business basis.

GROUCHO: How do you like that? Everytime I get romantic with you you want to talk business. There's something about me that brings out the business in every woman. . . . All right—we'll talk business. You see that man over there? Eating spaghetti?

8

The CAMERA PICKS UP *the* SPAGHETTI-EATER, *his face completely hidden by a mess of spaghetti.*

MRS. CLAYPOOL: No!

GROUCHO: Well, you see the spaghetti.

MRS. CLAYPOOL: Yes—

GROUCHO: Well, behind that spaghetti is none other than Arturo Guili, director of the New York Opera Company.

The spaghetti is lowered for a second; we see GUILI's *face.*

GROUCHO: Do you follow me?

MRS. CLAYPOOL *(eagerly)*: Yes.

GROUCHO: Well, stop following me or I'll have you arrested. Now! I have arranged for you to invest two hundred thousand dollars in the New York Opera Company.

MRS. CLAYPOOL: I don't understand.

GROUCHO: Don't you see? You'll be a patron of the opera. You'll get into society. Then you can marry me and they'll kick you *out* of society. All you lose is two hundred thousand dollars.

GUILI *comes into the scene.*

GUILI: Ah, Mr. Driftwood! Mr. Driftwood! *(He bows deeply)*

GROUCHO *(arising, imitating* GUILI, *bows deeply, and both* DRIFTWOOD *and* GUILI *continue bowing)*: Ah, Mr. Guili. . . . Mrs. Claypool, Mr. Guili, Mr. Guili, Mrs. Claypool, Mr. Guili. *(Stops bowing)* I could go on like this all night, but it's tough on my suspenders. Now, where was I? Oh, yes. Mr. Guili, Mrs. Claypool. Mrs. Guili, Mr. Claypool.

GUILI: Mrs. Claypool—*(Bends and kisses her hand)*

GROUCHO *(looking at her hand)*: I just wanted to see if your rings were still there.

GUILI *(looks at* MRS. CLAYPOOL*)*: Mrs. Claypool, you are as charming as you are beautiful.

MRS. CLAYPOOL: I'm afraid you've used that speech before, Mr. Guili.

GROUCHO: Yes, he said the same thing to me when I met him. Now, let's understand each other. Listen, Guili—making love to

9

Mrs. Claypool is my racket; all you're after is two hundred thousand dollars.

MRS. CLAYPOOL: By the way, Mr. Guili, what do you intend to do with the money?

GROUCHO: And you'd better make it sound plausible, because, incredible as it may seem, Mrs. Claypool isn't as big a sap as she looks. *(To* MRS. CLAYPOOL*)* How's that for love-making?

MRS. CLAYPOOL: I think the Italians do it better.

GROUCHO: All right, Guili it's your turn. And remember—you can't throw Mrs. Claypool down. At least, that's been my experience.

GUILI: Mrs. Claypool, it is most generous of you to help us. Now, then—you have of course heard of Rudolfo Lassparri?

MRS. CLAYPOOL: Of course.

GUILI: He is the greatest tenor since Caruso. Tonight, with the money you so generously provide, I sign Lassparri for the New York Opera. He will be a sensation, and society will be at your feet.

GROUCHO *(looking at* MRS. CLAYPOOL*'s feet)*: Well, there's plenty of room.

GUILI: And now—*(He consults his watch)*—the opera awaits us. If you will both honor me by occupying my box—

MRS. CLAYPOOL: I shall be charmed. *(She rises)*

GUILI: And you, Mr. Driftwood?

GROUCHO *(as the* WAITER *appears with the order)*: I'll be along later. And remember, Guili—lay off the love-making, because I saw Mrs. Claypool first. Of course her mother really saw her first, but that was before my time. See you later.

> GUILI *and* MRS. CLAYPOOL *depart; the* CAMERA *again* PICKS UP *the* BLONDE *at the adjoining table.*

GROUCHO: Hey, come on over. I've got another check for you.

OR

(To a PASSING WOMAN*)* Pardon me, Madam, did you drop this?

Fade out

10

Fade in:
Exterior, Opera House

All the excitement and glitter of the opening night. Automobiles and carriages driving up to the main entrance. Fashionably dressed people entering the Opera House.

Closer Angle—Main Entrance, *the crowd in the lobby.* GUILI *and* MRS. CLAYPOOL *among them.*

Gallery Entrance—Opera House, *a poorer, shabbier crowd, but an even happier one. Occasional members of the arriving audience singing loud snatches of the songs. Among them the* SHOP-KEEPER *and his expansive* FAMILY—*also the* STREET CLEANER. *Through all of this, the sound of an orchestra tuning up.*

Underneath the Stage, *the* ORCHESTRA *tuning up, preparatory to entering the pit.*

Backstage Stairs

The MEMBERS OF THE ENSEMBLE, *in costume, trooping down the stairs to take their places on the stage.*

The Camera Travels Up the Stairs, *showing the descending* TROUPE. *It shoots along the corridor and* STOPS *for a moment at a poster on the wall, which reads:*

OPERA COMPANY
—MILAN—
Presents
The World's Greatest Tenor
RUDOLFO LASSPARRI
And the following company
of distinguished artists:

The names of the distinguished artists, however, are in such small type that they cannot be read.

The CAMERA TRAVELS *a few feet farther and pauses to reveal: a dressing room door. On it is lettered simply:* RUDOLFO LASSPARRI.

Dissolve through the Door to:
Lassparri's Dressing Room

HARPO *is revealed—*HARPO *dressed as Pagliacci and very much the opera singer. He swings his arms wide; opens his mouth for a great note, but nothing comes out. He is greatly disappointed by this, pats his chest a few times, uses the atomizer, and tries again. Still nothing happens.*

Outside the Stage Door, *a waiting group of* GIRLS *as a limousine draws up.*

A GIRL: It's Lassparri!

Others pick up the cry: "Lassparri!" *A milling crowd as he steps out of his car. Autograph books.* "Sign mine, please!" "Oh, Signor Lassparri!" *He swaggers through to the stage door, signing as he goes.*

Harpo Again

With a fine tweezers he is plucking out his eyebrows, jumping with pain as he does so. The door opens and LASSPARRI *enters.*

LASSPARRI *(furious)*: What are you doing in my costume? Take it off immediately!

HARPO *quickly peels off the clown costume, revealing that he is dressed underneath in the naval regalia of Lieutenant Pinkerton, of* Madama Butterfly.

LASSPARRI: You—!

He strikes HARPO *in the face.* HARPO *reels; regains his balance, and gives a quick naval salute. Then he strips off the Pinkerton costume, as the* CAMERA PICKS UP LASSPARRI's *face for a moment. We see* LASSPARRI's *fury turn to amazement, then we* CUT BACK *to* HARPO. *It turns out that under the Pinkerton costume he is dressed as Marguerite, from* Faust.

LASSPARRI: Sapristi! Take that off! *(HARPO becomes femininely coy; he is reluctant to disrobe)* Take it off, I tell you!

HARPO is still coy; he shrinks away. LASSPARRI takes a threatening step toward him; HARPO runs away; circles the dressing-room chair. The effect that we want to achieve here is that of the city slicker bent on ruining the innocent country girl. HARPO continues to run around the chair, and as he does so he drops the costume, and is finally revealed in running pants.

LASSPARRI: Stand still! *(He picks up the Marguerite costume)* Where did you get this?

For answer, HARPO opens a closet door; a girl in lingerie runs out and escapes from the room.

LASSPARRI: You are no longer my dresser! You are fired! Get out! *(HARPO starts to go. LASSPARRI seizes a short whip from the wall and gives HARPO a quick lash)* Get out!

As HARPO opens the door, LASSPARRI strikes him with the whip again. This second lashing is observed by a GIRL who is just emerging from a dressing room across the hallway. She is already in costume; she stands with her hand on the knob of her door, drawing it shut, and lettered on this door, in letters not so imposing as those on the LASSPARRI door, is her name:

ROSA CASTALDI

Simultaneously the first strains of the overture are heard from downstairs.

LASSPARRI *(changing his mind)*: The overture! Come back! Make me up at once!

HARPO goes back into the room, closing the door behind him. The GIRL across the hall stands watching for a second, then makes up her mind. She opens her door again.

Inside Rosa's Room—as Rosa Enters, *a MAID is busy hanging up costumes. ROSA picks up a bunch of flowers. There is a CLOSE-UP of a card attached to them:* TO ROSA FROM RUDOLFO. *She indignantly throws the bouquet into the wastebasket.*

THE MAID: Signorina!

ROSA: I wouldn't wear Lassparri's flowers if they were the only ones in the world! *(There is a* KNOCK *on the door)* Come in! *(She snaps out the words)*

A good-looking young man comes into the room, already in costume for the evening's opera. His name, as we learn, is RICARDO BARONI.

RICARDO *(already through the door as she says* "Come in!"*)*: Oh, no! Not if you're going to use that tone. Now let's try the whole thing over again, and this time be a little more cordial. *(He goes out, closing the door behind him—again he* KNOCKS*)*

ROSA: Come in.

RICARDO *(entering)*: That's better. Now, let's do it once more—

ROSA: Ricardo, you're such a fool.

RICARDO: Now, what was it you wanted to see me about?

ROSA: Oh, I suppose I sent for *you.*

RICARDO: Well, you meant to—didn't she, Marie? *(An appeal to the* MAID, *who giggles a little)* Now, look! Here it is the last night of the season and I'm more in love with you than ever, and what are you going to do about it?

ROSA: Now, Ricardo, we'll have all summer to talk that over. Tonight we have to sing an opera.

RICARDO: Have to sing an opera! *You* have to sing! What am I? Just a glorified chorus boy.

ROSA *(genuinely)*: Don't say that, Rickie.

RICARDO: I've got to say it. And I've got something else to say. What are you doing tonight? Unless that big ham Lassparri has asked you first.

ROSA: He *has* asked me first, Ricardo.

RICARDO *(despondent)*: Just my luck.

ROSA: But I am dining with you!

RICARDO: Hurray! There will be champagne, music—*(He notices the flowers in the wastebasket)*—flowers. *(He quickly picks up the bouquet, sees the name of* RUDOLFO*)* No, no flowers! *(He throws them down)*

The Orchestra Pit, *the upraised arms of the* ORCHESTRA LEADER. *At a signal the* ORCHESTRA PLAYS *the opening strain of* Pagliacci; *the curtain starts to rise.*

A Shot of the Audience *in rapt attention as the opera begins.*

Guili's Box *he and* MRS. CLAYPOOL *are revealed.*

The Stage
> *An ensemble scene, in which* RICARDO *figures as a leader of the* VILLAGERS. *They are singing their heads off.*

Outside the Stage Door
> STAGE DOORMAN, *sitting in his chair against the wall,* HUMMING *to the* MUSIC, *which floats out from the stage.* CHICO *comes along.*

DOORMAN: Hello, Fiorello! What are *you* doing here? Thought you were working as a streetcar conductor.

CHICO: I make quick profit. I got off at the end of the line. . . . Where's Ricardo?

> CAMERA PANS *with* CHICO *as he goes backstage. Encounters* STAGEHAND.

STAGEHAND: Hello! Thought you were working on a farm. What happened?

CHICO: Oh, the same old story. The farmer's daughter.

STAGEHAND: Oh, the farmer had a daughter?

CHICO: No, he didn't have a daughter. That was the trouble . . . Ricardo!

> CHICO *proceeds farther. Encounters* HARPO. *Embrace and fond greeting.*

CHICO: Where is Ricardo?

> HARPO *points to stage.*

On Stage
> *Climax of the music.*

15

The Audience Again—*applauding.*

In the Wings—Backstage

> RICARDO *comes off stage, to find* CHICO *waiting for him. During the early lines of the scene the other singers are trooping past. The entire scene, of course, is played to an undercurrent of music.*

RICARDO *(in considerable surprise)*: Fiorello!

CHICO: Ricardo! *(They embrace)*

RICARDO: What are you doing here? I thought you were out with the circus.

CHICO: The circus? When was I with the circus? Oh, yes . . . I nearly forgot. That was a long time ago—last week. Since then I have had lots of jobs.

RICARDO: Doing anything now?

CHICO: Well, I was playing the piano in a Chinese restaurant, but the boss tried to pay me off in lichee nuts. I said "Lichee nuts to you, mister" and I quit.

RICARDO *(with a deep sigh)*: Your piano and my voice. All those years we studied at the conservatory, and what's come of it?

CHICO: What's the matter with you? We are still young, we have our health.

> *The voice of* LASSPARRI, *now* SINGING *on stage, swells to a climax. The* CAMERA CATCHES HIM *in action for a second, while* RICARDO *and* CHICO *turn and look at him. From the distance comes the* APPLAUSE *of the audience.*

CHICO: You hear that? Some day, Ricardo, you are where Lassparri is, and that applause is for you. When you were a little boy, six years old, you sing better than Lassparri. Remember those concerts we give in the church?

RICARDO: Maybe I was better at six than I am now.

CHICO: What you talk about? You are better than Lassparri *ever* was, and you *know* it.

RICARDO: All right—*I* know it, and *you* know it, but the public doesn't know it.

16

CHICO: Then we tell the public. You know what you need? You need a manager. Some wise guy. *(Slaps his thigh)* I know just the fellow.

RICARDO: You do? Who is it?

CHICO: Me!

RICARDO: But you wouldn't make any money at it.

CHICO: All right, I break even. As long as I don't lose anything. *(On stage* ROSA *begins to* SING. *Again the men turn and look)* It is our Rosa. *She* has done well. *(*RICARDO's *eyes are glued on the stage; he does not answer)* You are still crazy about her? *(*RICARDO *nods)* And she about you?

RICARDO: Even if she were, I couldn't ask her to marry me.

CHICO: You wait—everything come out all right. Anyhow, you and I—we are together again. Like old times, eh?

RICARDO: Like old times.

CHICO *(an arm around him)*: You betcha my life. Don't worry— the manager fix everything.

Curb in Front of Opera House, GROUCHO *drives up in cab.*

GROUCHO: Is the opera over yet?

CARRIAGE STARTER: Not yet, signor. A few minutes.

GROUCHO *(to* DRIVER*)*: I told you to slow those horses down. On account of you I nearly heard the opera. It's the narrowest escape I ever had in my life.

Interior, Opera House

LASSPARRI *is pouring out his voice in the golden notes of the final aria of the opera.*

The Stage, *as* LASSPARRI *finishes his song. The curtain drops. Thunders of* APPLAUSE *throughout the house.*

Shots Among the Audience—of Various Representative Groups

In the boxes wild applause from the people in evening dress.

In the galleries, mad enthusiasm. People standing up on their seats, cheering. Cries of "Bravo! Bravissima! Bis!" *Yells for* "Lassparri."

The SHOPKEEPER *and* HIS YOUNGSTERS—*the* STREET CLEANER—*yelling themselves hoarse in approval.*

The LEADER *of the orchestra taking a bow.*

LASSPARRI *taking several bows.* ROSA *takes two bows with him.*

The curtain finally dropping. The house lights flush full on; the footlights dim.

Main Entrance, Opera House, PEOPLE *are pouring out.*

Groucho's Cab—at Curb

DRIVER: She is over, signor, the opera!

GROUCHO: All right—here's my ticket. *(He gives it to the driver and dashes from the carriage into the Opera House, through the lobby. As he weaves his way through the people coming out, he shouts):* Bravo! Bravo! Bravo! *(Continuing to* SHOUT, *he disappears into the auditorium)*

Guili's Box

GUILI: Your good friend Mr. Driftwood does not seem to be an opera lover.

MRS. CLAYPOOL: I can't understand it. Where is he?

GUILI: If you will pardon my saying so, Mrs. Claypool, Mr. Driftwood seems to me hardly the person to handle your business affairs.

MRS. CLAYPOOL: I am beginning to think the same thing.

Groucho Arriving in Guili's Box

GUILI *is helping* MRS. CLAYPOOL *with her evening wrap.*

GROUCHO *(still applauding)*: Bravo! Bravo! *(He drops into a chair)* Well, I made it. How soon does the curtain go up?

GUILI: The curtain, Mr. Driftwood, will go up again next season.

18

MRS. CLAYPOOL: You have missed the entire opera.

GROUCHO: It's all right—I'll see the second show.

GUILI: Well, Mrs. Claypool, was I right? Isn't Rudolfo Lassparri the greatest tenor that ever lived?

MRS. CLAYPOOL: How much would you have to pay him?

GUILI: What is the difference? He must sail with us tomorrow night, no matter how much we pay him. He would be worth a thousand dollars a night.

GROUCHO: How much?

GUILI: A thousand dollars a night.

GROUCHO: What does he do?

GUILI: What does he *do*? He *sings*.

GROUCHO: Why, you can get a phonograph record of Minnie the Moocher for seventy-five cents. For a buck and a quarter you can get Minnie.

GUILI *(ignoring this)*: If you will excuse me, Mrs. Claypool, I think I had better arrange to see Lassparri. You are agreed? One thousand dollars a night?

MRS. CLAYPOOL: Whatever you think.

GROUCHO: A thousand dollars. *(To the* CAMERA*)* There must be some way for me to get a piece of that. *(To the others again)* Wait a minute—why don't *I* sign Lassparri? I represent Mrs. Claypool.

GUILI: But I represent the New York Opera Company. *(He hails a passing* USHER; *hands him a card)* Boy, will you give my card to Signor Lassparri, please?

GROUCHO: Ah—pardon me. I think I see a rat I used to know. *(He leaves)*

In the Wings, *a few privileged opera-goers have come back stage, and are congratulating the artists. Quite a few are clustered around* LASSPARRI; *they move away to the accompaniment of his gracious but condescending* "Thank you's." LASSPARRI *has a dressing gown over his costume. In another group stand* CHICO, ROSA, *and* RICARDO.

CHICO *(embracing* ROSA*)*: Our little Rosa! How you sang tonight!

The Lassparri Group Again

HARPO *stands there carrying a serving dish with a cover on it. He tries to get* LASSPARRI's *attention, but fails. Finally, right at* LASSPARRI's *ear, he gives a shrill whistle, fingers in mouth.* LASSPARRI *jumps.*

LASSPARRI: What is it? What do you want?

HARPO *stands formally at attention with the covered dish in hand. He tilts the cover a little, revealing a card underneath.* LASSPARRI *takes it.* HARPO *now tilts the cover at another angle and pulls out a sandwich. He disappears, eating it.* LASSPARRI *looks at the card.*

Insert of Card

Arturo Guili
Managing Director
New York Opera Company
Scribbled across the card are the words:
"May I see you? Important?"

Back to Scene

LASSPARRI *stands with the card in his hand, as* ROSA *and* RICARDO *pass by, laughing.* LASSPARRI *grasps her arm, taking her away from* RICARDO.

LASSPARRI: Ah, here you are. My good friend Arturo Guili is coming around. How would you like to have supper with us?

ROSA: I'm so sorry, Signor Lassparri. I already have an engagement.

LASSPARRI *(a look at* RICARDO*)*: Oh! I see. Well, that's too bad, because I have an idea he is going to invite me to sing in New York—and he may permit me to select my leading lady. . . . You—ah—you cannot break your engagement?

ROSA: I am terribly sorry, Signor. *(She walks away with* RICARDO*)*

Camera Pans with Lassparri

He stumbles over HARPO. *Business.*

LASSPARRI: You did that on purpose! You are fired! You understand! Fired! *(He strikes him—*GROUCHO *enters)*

GROUCHO: Hey, you big bully! What are you doing to that little bully?

LASSPARRI: What have you got to say about it?

GROUCHO: Just this: Are those tights red or have you got high blood pressure?

OR

Me? I don't even know you, and I'm not in the habit of speaking to people I don't know. If you have anything to say to me, get somebody to introduce us.

LASSPARRI *(with upraised arm)*: Why, you——(HARPO *quickly loosens a rope. There is a quick* CLOSE-UP *of a descending sandbag. It falls squarely on* LASSPARRI'S *head, knocking him cold)*

GROUCHO *(shaking hands with* HARPO*)*: Nice work! I think you got him. *(He looks at* LASSPARRI, *bends down and listens to his heart. Shakes his head dubiously.* HARPO *looks scared. Pulls out a bottle, uncorks it and places it before* LASSPARRI'S *nostrils)* Smelling salts, eh? Sorry for what you did, eh? Well, that shows a nice spirit.

LASSPARRI *begins to react, looks up dazedly and sits up.* HARPO *rushes over for another sandbag. It drops, knocking* LASSPARRI *out again.* HARPO *goes, waving farewell to* GROUCHO.

GROUCHO *drops some ashes on the unconscious* LASSPARRI *and puts one foot on the body, gladiator-style.*

GROUCHO: Get fresh with me, huh?

CHICO *enters.*

CHICO *(sizing up the situation)*: What's the matter, mister?

GROUCHO: Oh, we had a argument, and this fellow pulled a knife on me, so I shot him.

CHICO *(he lifts a foot, preparatory to putting it on* LASSPARRI'S *body)*: Do you mind if I—ah—?

GROUCHO: Help yourself, plenty of room.

CHICO *puts one foot on* LASSPARRI; GROUCHO'S *foot still rests there. In the minds of the boys,* LASSPARRI's *body immediately becomes a brass rail.*

GROUCHO: Two beers, bartender.

CHICO: I'll take two beers, too.

GROUCHO *(drifting right into that barroom conversation)*: Well, things seem to be getting better around the country.

CHICO: I don't know—I'm a stranger here myself.

GROUCHO *(looking at him curiously)*: Stranger? Aren't you an Italian?

CHICO: No, no. I just look that way because my mother and father are Italian.

GROUCHO: I just remembered—I came back here looking for somebody. You don't know who it is, do you?

CHICO: Funny—it just slipped my mind.

GROUCHO *(snapping his fingers)*: I remember now, the greatest tenor in the world! That's what I'm after!

CHICO: That's funny. I am his manager.

GROUCHO: Whose manager?

CHICO: The greatest tenor in the world.

GROUCHO: The fellow that sings at the opera here?

CHICO: Sure!

GROUCHO: What's his name?

CHICO: What do you care? Some Italian name—I can't pronounce it. What you want with him?

GROUCHO: Well, I'd like to offer him a job. Would he be interested?

CHICO: I don't know, but *I'm* interested. That's the main thing. What sort of job?

GROUCHO: With the New York Opera. America is waiting to hear him sing.

CHICO: Well, he can sing loud, but he can't sing that loud.

GROUCHO: Well, I think we can get America to meet him halfway. The main thing is, can he sail tomorrow night?

CHICO: If you pay him enough money, he can sail *last* night. How much you pay him?

22

GROUCHO *(aside)*: Let's see—a thousand dollars a night. I'm entitled to a little profit. *(To* CHICO*)* How about ten dollars a night?

    CHICO *laughs scornfully.*

CHICO: Ten dollars! . . . *(A quick change of mood)* All right. I'll take it.

GROUCHO: That's fine. Of course, I want a ten-per-cent commission for putting the deal over.

CHICO: And I get ten per cent as his manager.

GROUCHO: Well, that leaves eight dollars. Say he sings once a week—that's eight dollars a week clear profit for him.

CHICO *(considering a week)*: He sends five dollars home to his mother.

GROUCHO: Well, that still leaves him three dollars.

CHICO: Three dollars. Can he live in New York on that?

GROUCHO: Like a prince—of course, he won't be able to eat but he can live like a prince. Oh, I forgot to tell you. He'll have to pay income tax on that three dollars.

CHICO: Income tax?

GROUCHO: Yes, there's a federal tax and the state tax and there may be a city tax. And, naturally, a sales tax.

CHICO: How much does that all come to?

GROUCHO: Well, I figure if he doesn't sing too often, he can break even.

CHICO: All right. We'll take it.

GROUCHO: Fine! *(He pulls out two contracts)* Now just his name there and you sign at the bottom. You don't have to read yours because it's a duplicate.

CHICO: What?

GROUCHO: A duplicate. *(*CHICO *looks at him)* Don't you know what duplicates are?

CHICO: Oh, sure! Those five kids up in Canada.

GROUCHO: Well, I wouldn't know about that. I haven't been in Canada for years.

CHICO: Wait a minute. Before I sign anything, what does it say?

GROUCHO: Go ahead and read it.

CHICO (a little reluctantly): Well—er—you read it. I don't like to read anything unless I know what it says.

GROUCHO (catching on): I see. All right, *I'll* read it to you. Can you hear?

CHICO: I haven't heard anything yet. Did you say anything?

GROUCHO: Well, I haven't said anything worth hearing.

CHICO: I guess that's why I didn't hear anything.

GROUCHO (having the last word): Well, that's why I didn't say anything. (He scans the contract, holding it near him and then far away. CHICO watches him suspiciously)

CHICO: Wait a minute. Can *you* read?

GROUCHO (holding contract farther and farther away): I can read, but I can't see it. If my arms were a little longer, I could read it. . . . Ah, here we are. Now pay attention to this first clause. (Reads) "The party of the first part shall be known in this contract as the party of the first part." How do you like that. Pretty neat, eh?

CHICO: No, that'sa no good.

GROUCHO (indignantly): What's the matter with it?

CHICO (conciliatorily): I don't know—let's hear it again.

GROUCHO: "The party of the first part shall be known in this contract as the party of the first part."

CHICO: It sounds a little better this time.

GROUCHO: Well, it grows on you. Want to hear it once more?

CHICO: Only the first part.

GROUCHO: The *party* of the first part?

CHICO: No. The *first part* of the party of the first part.

GROUCHO: Well, it says "The first part of the party of the first part shall be known in this contract"—look! Why should we quarrel about a thing like that? (He tears off the offending clause) We'll take it right out.

CHICO (tearing the same clause out of his contract): Sure, it's too long anyhow. Now what have we got left?

24

GROUCHO: Well, I've got about a foot and a half. . . . Now, then: "The party of the second part shall be known in this contract as the party of the second part."

CHICO: Well, I don't know. I don't like the second party, either.

GROUCHO: You should have come to the first party. We didn't get home till around four in the morning. *(Slight pause)* I was blind for three days.

CHICO: Look, couldn't the first part of the second party be the second part of the first party? Then we got something.

GROUCHO: Look! Rather than go through all that again, what do you say? *(He indicates a willingness to tear further)*

CHICO: Fine. *(They both tear off another piece)*

GROUCHO: Now, I've got something here you're *bound* to like. You'll be crazy about it.

CHICO: No, I don't like it.

GROUCHO: You don't like what?

CHICO: Whatever it is.

GROUCHO: All right. Why should we break up an old friendship over a thing like this? Ready?

CHICO: Okay. *(They both tear)* Now, the next part I don't think *you're* going to like.

GROUCHO: All right—your word's good enough for me. *(They both tear)* Now then, is *my* word good enough for *you*?

CHICO: I should say not.

GROUCHO: All right—let's go. *(They both tear.* GROUCHO *looking at the contract)* The party of the eighth part—

CHICO: No. *(They tear)*

GROUCHO: The party of the ninth part—

CHICO: No. *(They tear)* Say, how is it I got a skinnier contract than you?

GROUCHO: I don't know. You must have been out on a tear last night. Anyhow, now we're all set. Now sign right here. *(He produces a fountain pen)*

CHICO: I forgot to tell you. I can't write.

GROUCHO: That's all right. There's no ink in the pen, anyway. But, listen, it's a bargain, isn't it? We've got a contract, no matter how small it is.

CHICO (extending hand. GROUCHO clasps it): You betcha! Only one thing I want to know: what does this say? (Showing last piece of contract left)

GROUCHO: Oh, that's nothing. That's the usual clause in every contract. It says if any of the parties participating in the contract are shown not to be in their right mind, the contract is nullified.

CHICO: What do you call it?

GROUCHO: That's what they call a sanity clause.

CHICO: You can't fool me. There ain't no sanity clause!

Guili Coming Backstage

As he enters the scene, GROUCHO *crosses to him.*

GROUCHO: Well, Guili, if you want your tenor, you've got to do business with me.

GUILI: What do you mean?

GROUCHO: I mean that I've signed him up personally, and if you want him you'll have to pay. And I'm not going to let him go for any measly thousand dollars a performance. I'm asking fifteen hundred.

GUILI: I don't believe it! Lassparri wouldn't sign with an unknown like you.

GROUCHO: Well, he has. (*Turns to* CHICO, *who has just entered the scene*) Hasn't he?

CHICO: No. You signed Ricardo Baroni—that's my man . . . Baroni. You must get the name wrong.

GUILI: Baroni! Who is Baroni? (*He begins to laugh at* GROUCHO's *discomfiture*)

GROUCHO (*to* CHICO): That's a fine way to behave! Here I come in and make an honest business deal with you and you try to cheat me. And what for? A few paltry dollars. For eight dollars a week. You ought to be ashamed of yourself. (*He tears up contract*) I'm through with you. Look at me. I was trying to skin you out of nearly a thousand dollars a week. That's more like it.

CHICO: I do you big favor. Baroni sing better than Lassparri ever sing. He is real artist.

GROUCHO: That's not the point. I asked you for Lassparri! Now where is he?

Lassparri's Body

He moves a little. Obviously he is regaining consciousness. We see the expressions of the various people.

GUILI: Lassparri!

GROUCHO *(to* CHICO*)*: Lassparri?

CHICO: Sure. That's Lassparri.

GROUCHO: That's all I need to make it a perfect day. Come on, let's get out of here.

CHICO: Yes, I think a walk will do us good. *(He follows* GROUCHO, *who starts to leave)*

We see GUILI *kneeling before* LASSPARRI, *tenderly raising his head. A hand releases the rope again. The descending bag knocks* LASSPARRI *and* GUILI *cold. It has all been very fast. We now see a flash of* HARPO, *his hand just leaving the rope.*

CHICO: Good shot, Tomasso!

GROUCHO: Won't you join us in a walk?

HARPO takes GROUCHO'S *arm and they walk out, followed by* CHICO. RICARDO, *whistling, comes into the scene.* CHICO *stops him.*

CHICO: Ricardo, I got good news for you!

RICARDO *(elated)*: Yes?

CHICO: I just missed getting you a job by that much. *(He indicates a small amount of space between his fingers)*

RICARDO: You did? With whom?

CHICO: This man. *(Indicating* GROUCHO*)* He's my friend. We all his friends.

GROUCHO *(looking at him)*: Something tells me I'm going to regret that I ever met you.

CHICO: I think so too. Eh, Tomasso?
They laugh together.

Fade out

Fade in:
The Dock and the Boat—Night
The confusion of the dock just before a sailing, with passengers arriving; trunks being wheeled past, etc.

The Gangplank, PASSENGERS *streaming aboard. We hear the* MUSIC *of the* SHIP'S ORCHESTRA.

The Ticket Window on the Dock, *a line of* PASSENGERS *surrendering their tickets.*

The Gangplank Again
The CAMERA CENTERS *on* GROUCHO *and* MRS. CLAYPOOL *as they move up the gangplank.*
MRS. CLAYPOOL *(to* GROUCHO, *who is following her with bags)*: Are you sure you *have* everything, Otis?
GROUCHO: I've never had any complaints yet.

On the Dock
The CAMERA PICKS OUT ROSA *and* RICARDO.
RICARDO: Well, here you are. On your way to America, and fame.
ROSA: Oh, Rickie, I wish you were going with me.
RICARDO: Well, I would if I had the fare. Say, that reminds me. I forgot to bring you those flowers.
ROSA: What flowers?
RICARDO: I saw the most beautiful flowers—in the park. And if that cop hadn't been watching, they'd be here now.
ROSA: Oh, Ricardo, I'm going to miss you.
RICARDO: How do you think I feel about it?
     GUILI *comes along.*
GUILI: Ah, Miss Castaldi! All ready for the big trip?

28

ROSA: Oh, Mr. Guili. This is Ricardo Baroni, of the opera company.

RICARDO: How do you do?

GUILI: Baroni? Did you say Baroni? *(He laughs)*

RICARDO: What's so funny about that?

GUILI *(through his laughter)*: Mr. Otis B. Driftwood seemed to think that you had quite a voice.

ROSA: Oh, he has, Mr. Guili—really he has. A wonderful voice.

RICARDO: Really, I have.

GUILI: Well, that's very interesting. Very in- —Ah, Rudolfo!

This as LASSPARRI *comes along the dock, escorted by most of the* OPERA COMPANY, *all very gay. They bring an accordion, a guitar, etc. A great exchange of greetings:* "Hello!" "Hello!" "Rosa!" "Come on, we take you aboard!"

ROSA *(as she is swept up the gangplank)*: Come on, Rickie!

LASSPARRI: Well, Rosa! Here we are! On our way! *(He puts an arm around her)*

Close-up—Ricardo

He sees LASSPARRI *and* ROSA *together. He feels very much out of it.*

Top of the Gangplank

The gay CROWD *reaches the deck. Cries of* "Viva Lassparri!" *from the dock.* LASSPARRI *turns, acknowledges the greeting by lifting his hat; shows the bandaged head.*

LASSPARRI: Already they miss me!

GUILI: It is the fortune of war. Italy's loss is America's gain.

The CROWD *around* LASSPARRI *begins to beseech him.* "Come on, Lassparri! A farewell song!" "Yes, Lassparri!! A song! A song!"

LASSPARRI: Oh, I must beg to be excused. I have a slight touch of laryngitis. *(He turns to* GUILI*)* Why should I sing when I am not paid for it?

The CROWD *groans its disappointment. Someone says:* "How about Rosa?" "Yes, Rosa!" "You sing, Rosa!"

They surround ROSA, *who is scanning the crowd, looking for* RICARDO. *Then her gaze goes to the dock. She finds him, and waves to him.*

Ricardo on the Dock, *as he waves back.*

The Deck Again, *more beseeching from the* CROWD.
ROSA: Why, of course. I'll be very happy to.
A shout of pleasure as they strike up a tune with their musical instruments. She SINGS.
RICARDO SINGS *back to her—a second chorus. The next few scenes are played under cover of the* SINGING.
ROSA *(to* GUILI*)*: Mr. Guili! Hasn't he a wonderful voice? Couldn't you use him in New York?
GUILI: It is not a bad voice. Some day, perhaps, when he has made a reputation.

A Sailor Ringing the Departure Bell
"All visitors ashore!" "All visitors ashore!"

The Gangplank
Visitors streaming down.

On Deck Again
CHICO *and* HARPO *arrive.*
CHICO: Rosa! We look all over for you! *(He embraces her)*
ROSA: Good-by, Fiorello! *(*HARPO *embraces her)* Good-by, Tomasso!
HARPO *comes out of the embrace; is about to start all over again, but* RICARDO *beats him to it.*
We hear the bell RINGING *again.*
HARPO *goes around the deck, embracing one girl after another. The final one turns out to be a middle-aged woman.*

30

HARPO *starts to swing on her.* CHICO *and* BARONI *enter the scene.*

CHICO: Come on! We gotta get off! (HARPO *points to an additional group of girls*) It's all right—I kiss them already. Come on!

The three start to run off.

The Passengers' Gangplank

UNIFORMED OFFICER: All right! Let her go!

SAILORS *start to pull in the gangplank.*

GROUCHO *suddenly appears on the deck—frantic.*

GROUCHO: Wait a minute. Have I got time to go back and pay my hotel bill?

OFFICER: Too late!

GROUCHO: That's fine. (*He rushes away*)

A Corridor on the Boat

A STEWARD *wheeling a trunk on a truck.*

Farther Along the Corridor

GROUCHO *squeezing against the wall as the* STEWARD *wheels the trunk past.*

GROUCHO: Hey, that's my trunk! Where are you going with that?

STEWARD: Suite Number Fifty-eight.

GROUCHO: That's me. (*He vaults up onto the trunk and is wheeled along with it*)

Another Spot in the Corridor

GROUCHO *and his trunk are still being wheeled along. From around a corner comes a* STEWARD *with another load of luggage, piled high. Not seeing where he is going, he bumps into* GROUCHO's *trunk.*

GROUCHO: Hey, you! Why don't you look where you're going? I had my hand out.

SECOND STEWARD: I'm sorry, sir.

31

GROUCHO *(jumps down and examines the front of his trunk):* Sorry? Look at that fender—it's all bumped out of shape. What's your number?

There is a CLOSE-UP *of the man's badge, which* GROUCHO *reads.*

Back to Scene

GROUCHO: Thirty-two. You'll pay for this, my good man. Are you insured?

SECOND STEWARD *(pardonably confused):* What?

GROUCHO: Have you got any insurance?

SECOND STEWARD: No, sir.

GROUCHO: Then you're just the fellow I want to see. *(He pulls a sheaf of papers out of his pocket)* I have here a liability policy which will absolutely protect you no matter what happens. If you lose a leg we'll help you look for it. Now, all this will cost you is— *(He notices a bill peeping out of the man's pocket)* What have you got there? A dollar? *One* dollar. Thank you. *(He takes the dollar and sticks the paper into the man's pocket in its place)*

We get a QUICK CLOSE-UP—*the paper*

It is GROUCHO's *hotel bill. The part that is visible reads as follows:*

HOTEL ITALIA, MILAN
Otis B. Driftwood . . . . . 6000 lira.
IMMEDIATE PAYMENT REQUESTED.

Back to Scene

GROUCHO *(bounds back onto his trunk and addresses his own* STEWARD*):* All right—let's go. Suite Number Fifty-eight, and don't go over twenty miles an hour.

Close-up—a Stateroom Door on which Is Lettered:
SUITE A-B-C

The CAMERA DRAWS BACK, *revealing the ship's* PURSER, *talking to three distinguished-looking* MEN IN UNIFORM, *who look exactly alike. They are hung with medals; they have pointed black beards, one like the other, and they stand in a perfectly straight line.*

At the same moment GROUCHO *comes into view, perched on his trunk.*

THE PURSER (*throwing open the stateroom door*): Here you are, gentlemen—the finest suite on the boat.

The THREE MEN *enter the room, followed by the* PURSER.

The door closes; again we see the lettering: SUITE A-B-C

GROUCHO: Was that three fellows, or one fellow with three beards?

Another Corridor—an Angle Shot of Several Cabins, *their doors standing open.* GROUCHO, *on his trunk, comes into view; he is singing "Ridi, Pagliacci" lustily. The* CAMERA PANS *with him and stops at the first of the open doors. It is Cabin Number Fifty, occupied by* GUILI. *The door is standing open and* GUILI *is inside, combing his hair.* GROUCHO'*s voice draws him to the door.*

GROUCHO (*as he passes*): Ah, Mr. Guili! Signing any tenors today?

GUILI, *in annoyance, slams the door.* GROUCHO *continues right on his way, still singing.*

Cabin Number Fifty-two is next. LASSPARRI *is inside, surveying a still wounded head in the mirror.*

GROUCHO: I see you've still got a hangover. (*He goes right back into his song*)

LASSPARRI *turns quickly, sees who it is, grabs an ashtray and hurls it at* GROUCHO'*s head.* GROUCHO *catches the tray; uses it for cigar ashes. By good luck,* GROUCHO *has just reached that spot in the music where* PAGLIACCI LAUGHS. *So* GROUCHO LAUGHS, *tauntingly.*

The truck has not stopped moving for the LASSPARRI *scene. It now comes to Cabin Number Fifty-four, the door of which is closed. As* GROUCHO *reaches it the sound of* SOBBING *comes from within.*

33

GROUCHO: Pull up here, driver.

He jumps down; listens again; again we hear the SOBBING. *He* KNOCKS SOFTLY *on the door, waits a moment, then gently opens it.* ROSA *is inside—*SOBBING *on the bed.*

GROUCHO *goes to her; puts a comforting hand on her shoulder. She looks up.*

GROUCHO: Anything I can do?

ROSA *(shakes her head)*: Just a little homesick.

GROUCHO: That's funny. I happen to have with me the greatest remedy for homesickness you ever saw. A fellow gave it to me just before the boat sailed. *(She giggles a little through her tears.* GROUCHO *has pulled a piece of paper out of his pocket)* Here's the recipe, and take it every two hours.

ROSA *opens the note.*

Insert

Some day I'll find you. *(Or whatever the key phrase of the song may be)*

Yours forever,

Ricardo.

Back to Scene:

ROSA's *tears change to smiles. She impulsively throws her arms around* GROUCHO *and kisses him. He goes cockily out of the cabin, once more* SINGING *"Pagliacci," and with a new spirit, mounts the trunk.*

Camera Follows Groucho to Next Cabin, Number Fifty-six

GROUCHO *(waving to* MRS. CLAYPOOL, *who can be glimpsed inside the room, taking cosmetic bottles out of a suitcase)*: Hello, Toots!

AS GROUCHO's TRUNK STOPS *we see that* MRS. CLAYPOOL *is installed in huge, luxurious quarters. As she turns to see who it is,* GROUCHO *comes into the room and surveys it.*

GROUCHO: Ah! *(He looks at one of the beds)* Twin beds! You little rascal, you!

Mrs. Claypool (apologetically): Well—that one is a day bed.

Groucho: A likely story! . . . Well, call me at nine o'clock. Good night. (He lies on the bed)

Mrs. Claypool: Will you please get off that bed, Mr. Driftwood! What will people say?

Groucho: They'll probably say you're a very lucky woman. Now, will you shut up and let me go to sleep?

Mrs. Claypool: No, I will not shut up! You will kindly get up at once!

Groucho: All right—I'll make you another proposition. Let's go into my room and talk the situation over.

Mrs. Claypool: What situation?

Groucho: Well, you've got me there. I tell you—you come to my room and I'll guarantee there'll *be* a situation. If not, I'm not the man I used to be.

Mrs. Claypool: I shall certainly not go to your room!

Groucho: All right—then I'll stay here.

Mrs. Claypool: All right, all right—I'll come. Only get out.

Groucho (jumping up): That's more like it. Shall we say—(The eyebrows)—ten minutes?

Mrs. Claypool (anything for peace): Yes. Ten minutes. Anything.

Groucho: Mrs. Claypool, you have made yourself a very happy woman. I shall be waiting—alone. And I might add in passing that if you're not there in ten minutes, I'll be here in eleven. And if I come in here again, Mrs. Claypool, there will be no beating around the bush.

Mrs. Claypool (beaten): All right, I promise to come. But please consider my reputation.

Groucho: Mrs. Claypool, I give you my word there will be nobody there but me. Nobody will see you go in, and if you stay there nobody will see you come out. And I can assure you, my pretty wench, that if you come to my room nothing will happen—unless you come to my room. (Exits, SINGING)

In the Hallway

The STEWARD *has already moved along to Cabin Number Fifty-eight. The* CAMERA FOLLOWS GROUCHO *as he does likewise. He arrives there just as the* STEWARD *is throwing open the door.*

STEWARD: Your cabin, signor.

GROUCHO peers in. To say that it is the smallest cabin in the world is to give it a break. There is a single bunk, which is about three feet long.

GROUCHO: Wait a minute—this can't be my room.

STEWARD: Yes, sir. Suite Number Fifty-eight.

GROUCHO: Fifty-eight—that's an awful big number for a rat-trap this size. *(While the* STEWARD *puts the trunk in place, he keeps talking)* Say, I'm lucky I didn't bring my *big* trunk. *(As* STEWARD *is through)* I'll have to have another room. This may be all right for a honeymoon couple, but I'm traveling alone.

STEWARD: I'm sorry, sir, but this is the only room left.

GROUCHO: This is an outrage! How did they come to put me in a room like this?

STEWARD: Mr. Guili picked it out for you, sir.

GROUCHO: Mr. Guili, eh? Well, I'll have to have my appendix taken out before I can get in there. Is there a doctor in the house?

STEWARD *(coming out into hall)*: Oh, I'm sure you'll find it very cozy, sir. Anything else, sir?

GROUCHO: Yes, tomorrow you can come and take the truck out—and *I'll* go in.

The STEWARD *goes.* GROUCHO *enters the room, humming "The Prisoner's Song" and opens the trunk. But the contents are not quite as expected. On one side crouches* RICARDO BARONI; *on the other, squeezed into an impossible space, is* CHICO. *Below* CHICO *a small drawer keeps him from properly utilizing his half of the trunk. Startled,* GROUCHO *leaps on the bunk as the two come out of their cramped quarters.*

CHICO: Hello, boss! Here we are again!

GROUCHO: I'm terribly sorry—I thought this was my trunk.

CHICO: It *is* your trunk.

GROUCHO: I don't remember packing you boys.

CHICO: You know Ricardo, the greatest tenor in the world. You sign him up once.

GROUCHO: Oh, sure—I just delivered a letter for you. How are you?

Both RICARDO *and* CHICO *have now emerged from their quarters, further jamming the room.*

RICARDO: Pretty good. A little cramped.

GROUCHO: I'm awfully sorry. If I'd known you boys were coming I would have got a bigger trunk. But if I'd got a bigger trunk I couldn't have got it into this room.

CHICO: It's all right. We taka pot luck.

GROUCHO *(examining shirt* CHICO *has on)*: Pardon me—isn't that my shirt you're wearing?

CHICO: I don't know—I found it in the trunk.

GROUCHO: Then it couldn't be mine. Well, it's a great pleasure to meet you boys again, but I was expecting my other suit. You didn't happen to see it, did you?

CHICO: Oh, sure. But it take up too much room. We sell it.

GROUCHO: Did you get anything for it?

CHICO: A dollar-forty.

GROUCHO: That was my suit all right. . . . Well, I think I put a shirt in this drawer. *(He opens the drawer;* HARPO *is curled up inside, in pajamas, and sound asleep)* That can't be my shirt. My shirt doesn't snore.

CHICO: Sssh! Don't wake him up. He's got insomnia and he's trying to sleep it off.

GROUCHO *backs away as* CHICO *and* RICARDO *help* HARPO, *still asleep, out of trunk and put him on the bunk.*

GROUCHO: Now tell me—I don't want to be inquisitive, but what are you fellows doing in my trunk?

CHICO: Itsa very simple. Ricardo love Rosa. She go to New York; we all go, too. We got no money, so we hide in trunk.

GROUCHO: Well, if you've got no money what are you going to do in New York.

RICARDO: I'm going to sing. There must be some place I can work. And I can be near Rosa—that's the main thing. You won't give us away, will you, Mr. Driftwood?

GROUCHO: Well, you picked a good place to hide. As long as you stay in this room, they'll never find you. You can't see this room except under a microscope.

RICARDO: It certainly is a small room.

GROUCHO: It *is* a little crowded, but in a pinch you can always go back in the trunk. Right now I wish you'd get out of here and stay out. I've got a date with a lady, and you know the old saying! two's company, but five's a crowd.

CHICO: We go, but first we got to eat. We no eat nothing all day, so we're hungry.

GROUCHO: Well, that sounds logical, but the main thing is that you've got to get out of here. We'll take the food situation up later.

CHICO (*very definitely*): We get food or we don't go.

GROUCHO (*a baleful glare at* CHICO): I knew I never should have met you boys. All right, but you've got to scram right out after you've eaten. And see if you can get those pajamas off that sleeping beauty. I've got other plans for those pajamas. (*He goes out*)

Cut to:
Groucho Opens Door, Exiting to Corridor

GROUCHO's STEWARD *is passing by.*

GROUCHO: Good evening, steward. What have you got for dinner?

STEWARD: Anything you like, sir. How about starting with some tomato juice? Or grape juice, pineapple juice, orange juice—

GROUCHO: Hey! Turn off the juice before I get electrocuted. I tell you. I'll have two fried eggs, two scrambled eggs, two soft-boiled eggs, two poached eggs—

CHICO (*from cabin*): And two hard-boiled eggs.

GROUCHO: And two hard-boiled eggs. (*HARPO still apparently asleep,* TOOTS *his horn)* Better make that three hard-boiled eggs. And some roast beef, rare, medium, well done and overdone—

CHICO: And two hard-boiled eggs.

GROUCHO: And two hard-boiled eggs. *(HARPO's horn again)* Make that three hard-boiled eggs. *(Another* TOOT *of the horn)* And one duck egg. By the way, have you any stewed prunes?

STEWARD: Yes, sir.

GROUCHO: Well, give 'em some black coffee—that'll sober 'em up.

CHICO: And two hard-boiled eggs.

HARPO's horn TOOTS *in rapid succession.*

GROUCHO: It's either very foggy out or make that twelve more hard-boiled eggs. And steward, rush that along, because the faster it comes the faster this convention will be over.

STEWARD: Yes, sir.

GROUCHO *(as* STEWARD *is about to go)*: Oh, steward, do they allow tipping on this boat?

STEWARD *(eagerly)*: Oh, yes, sir.

GROUCHO *(digging in pocket)*: Have you two fives?

STEWARD *(digging for change)*: Oh, yes, sir.

GROUCHO: Well, come back later—I've got a tenor in my trunk. *(STEWARD goes. GROUCHO goes back to cabin)*

As Groucho Enters Cabin, *the phone* RINGS *and* CHICO *answers it hurriedly.*

CHICO: Hello. Yes. *(He hangs up and turns to* GROUCHO*)* That was for you.

GROUCHO: I'm glad you told me. *(There is a* KNOCK *on the door.* GROUCHO *opens it. Two* MAIDS *stand outside)* Yes?

MAIDS: We've come to make up your room, sir.

CHICO: Are those my hard-boiled eggs?

GROUCHO: I can't tell till they get in the room. *(To* MAIDS*)* Come on in, girls, and leave all hope behind. But you've got to get out in ten minutes, so you'll have to work fast. *(MAIDS enter with cleaning things, vacuum cleaner, etc.* HARPO*, still asleep, immediately gets up and embraces one of the* MAIDS*. She struggles in* *vain. To* HARPO) There's a little misunderstanding here. I said *she* had to work fast, not you.

CHICO: It's no good talking to him. He's asleep.

GROUCHO: He does better asleep than I do awake. *(*ENGINEER *opens door and comes in)* Yes?

ENGINEER: I'm the engineer. I came to turn on the heat.

GROUCHO *(to* CAMERA*)*: Is it my imagination, or is it getting crowded in here?

> *A knock at the door.* GROUCHO *opens it. A* MANICURIST *with complete outfit is there.*

MANICURIST: Did you want a manicure?

GROUCHO: No—come on in.

> *She comes in, puts her tray and chair down. As she sits,* HARPO *thrusts his foot into her lap.* GROUCHO *extends his hand.*

MANICURIST *(to* GROUCHO*)*: Do you want your nails long or short?

GROUCHO: Better make 'em short. It's getting a little congested in here.

> *And it* is *pretty congested. The picture is* HARPO *struggling with one* MAID, *the other* MAID *is struggling with the vacuum cleaner and* CHICO, RICARDO *has finally found a little space on top of the trunk where he sits as comfortably as he can, reading a newspaper, the* ENGINEER *is* POUNDING *away at the pipes.*
>
> *A* KNOCK *at the door.* GROUCHO *opens it and sees a* GIRL.

GIRL: Pardon me, is my Aunt Minnie in here?

GROUCHO: No, but you can come in and prowl around. You can probably find somebody just as good.

> *She comes in, looks around and struggles toward the phone, and immediately begins* TALKING *into the transmitter. Luckily, the confusion is such that we can't hear her. It would probably turn out to be one of the dumbest conversations on record. Another* KNOCK *at the door and the* ENGINEER'S ASSISTANT *comes in.*

ASSISTANT: I'm the engineer's assistant. I came to turn off the heat.

GROUCHO: Why, I didn't know you cared. *(to* CAMERA*)* This is getting to be like Noah's ark. *(A* SCRUBWOMAN *enters, and goes*

unconcernedly about her work. Again to CAMERA*)* And I had a
date to be alone. *(Another* KNOCK *at the door.* FOUR STEWARDS
arrive, laden with food. GROUCHO *peers out at them)* You'll have
to come in one at a time. *(He indicates* ONE STEWARD, *who is
enormously fat)* And *you* can't come in at all, or I'm no judge of
distance.
CHICO: Food! Food!

> *As the* STEWARDS *enter,* RICARDO *scurries off the trunk and*
> CHICO *makes a dive for his hard-boiled eggs.* HARPO, *who has
> somehow managed to be lifted up in the air, supported by the
> other occupants, gets a scissors-hold on the neck of* ONE OF
> THE STEWARDS *and reaches for some food, his eyes still closed.
> In the ensuing melee, several* OTHER PASSENGERS *enter and
> a* STEWARD *with a suitcase or two.*

Mrs. Claypool *emerges from her cabin. She looks carefully around,
makes sure no one is there and puts her hand on the door of*
GROUCHO'S *stateroom. By this time* GROUCHO *has been forced
against the wall, with a* GIRL *pressing closely against him. As*
MRS. CLAYPOOL *opens the door,* GROUCHO *and the* GIRL *are
catapulted out,* GROUCHO *landing on* MRS. CLAYPOOL, *and
the* GIRL *on top of them.*
GROUCHO: Now, Mrs. Claypool, I can explain everything.

Fade out

Fade in:
Written Title—The Last Night Aboard
> *The* MUSIC *behind the title is gay, and the carnival spirit is
> carried out in the title decorations—horns being blown, paper
> hats, confetti, etc.*

Cut to:
Long Shot—Boat
> *Brilliantly lit from stem to stern, it is ploughing through the
> water. A* SEARCHLIGHT HITS THE BOAT. *Coming, apparently,*

from a passing boat, it travels up and down the Italian liner. The searchlight halts. It comes to a stop on the lower quarters of the boat. The CAMERA MOVES UP *to concentrate on this spot.*

Dissolve through to:
Interior

We are in the steerage. A gay and colorful Italian CROWD— *but obviously the poorer classes.* SINGING, DANCING, PLAYING *various* MUSICAL INSTRUMENTS. *Little groups eating, sitting on the floor.*

Cut to:
The Searchlight Again

It travels up the boat until it hits the top deck.

Dissolve through to:
Interior, Main Dining Room

It is another gay CROWD—*but these are first-class passengers in evening dress. Paper hats are perched on their heads; a handful of confetti is thrown, etc.*

The CAMERA *first shows the room as a whole—a great horseshoe table has been set up, and a hundred or more* PASSENGERS *are seated around it.*

As the CAMERA MOVES UP *we locate our principals—the* CAPTAIN *in the center of the horseshoe, flanked by the* THREE AVIATORS. *Also present are* LASSPARRI, ROSA, GROUCHO, MRS. CLAYPOOL, *and* GUILI, *in that order. An* ORCHESTRA *is* PLAYING; *dinner is still being served.*

The CAMERA, *after sweeping around the principals, returns to the* CAPTAIN *and the* AVIATORS.

Captain Getting to His Feet

APPLAUSE.

CAPTAIN: Ladies and gentlemen, I do not want the evening to pass without paying a little tribute to our distinguished guests of honor.

42

(With a wave of the hand he indicates the THREE AVIATORS, *who rise and bow to* APPLAUSE*)* The three greatest aviators in the world.

APPLAUSE *as they all sit.*

Mrs. Claypool, Guili, and Groucho

MRS. CLAYPOOL *(addressing* GUILI*)*: Isn't it all wonderful? After all, there's nothing like the last night of an ocean voyage.

GROUCHO: You bet your life there isn't. And you know why? Because it's the last time you're ever going to see those passengers you promised to look up in New York.

The CAMERA SHIFTS *to* LASSPARRI *and* ROSA.

LASSPARRI: But does it mean nothing to you that I am the greatest singer in the world?

ROSA *(apparently with complete innocence)*: But I love to hear you sing, Rudolfo.

LASSPARRI *(annoyed)*: No, no! I do not mean singing.

ROSA: But you said singing, Rudolfo.

LASSPARRI: But I don't *mean* singing.

ROSA: Then what *do* you mean?

LASSPARRI: Surely you don't expect me to say what I mean! If I said what I mean you would leave immediately.

ROSA *(stringing him along)*: Well, if you think I *should*—*(She starts to rise)*

LASSPARRI *(clutching her arm)*: No, no, no! What a woman! Let me put it this way: I love you! I adore you! I would die for you! Now, do you understand?

ROSA: I'm afraid not.

The CAMERA MOVES *to include* GROUCHO.

GROUCHO: This is the silliest conversation I ever listened to. The whole thing is very simple. When he says he's the greatest singer in the world, that means he loves you. Personally, I don't believe *either* statement.

The CAMERA CONCENTRATES *on* ROSA *and* GROUCHO, *leaving out* LASSPARRI.

ROSA: There may be something in what you say.

43

GROUCHO: I'll tell you something confidentially. The only tenor I could ever stand was a fellow called Ricardo Baroni. Ever hear of him?

ROSA: Ricardo! I wonder where he is right now. Probably roaming over the countryside some place. Ricardo loves the open. He never could stand being cooped up.

GROUCHO: He still doesn't like it.

Groucho's Room

The trunk slowly opens; HARPO's face emerges. He comes out; opens the door and cautiously investigates the corridor. He finds the path clear, WHISTLES to the others to follow him.

CHICO (to RICARDO): Come on. We find something to eat.

RICARDO: Are you sure it's safe? If they catch us they'll deport us.

CHICO: What have we got to lose? If they deport us they got to feed us. Letsa take a chance.

They start to tiptoe out.

Guili and Mrs. Claypool

GUILI: Ah, yes, I too have suffered. It is now five years since my beloved wife passed on.

MRS. CLAYPOOL: Mr. Claypool went to his reward three years ago.

GUILI: And left you all alone. *(She nods sadly)* With eight million dollars.

MRS. CLAYPOOL *(with a sigh)*: Eight million dollars.

The CAMERA MOVES to include GROUCHO.

GROUCHO: Listen, Guili, this'll do you no good. If Mrs. Claypool wants to marry a fortune hunter, she's always got me.

Close-up—Groucho Alone

GROUCHO: And I'll tell you another thing. You can't exactly call me a fortune hunter, because when I first proposed to Mrs. Claypool I thought she only had seven million . . . But the extra million has never interfered with my feelings for her.

Mrs. Claypool and Groucho

MRS. CLAYPOOL: If you have any real feeling for me, Mr. Driftwood, you will stop associating with the kind of riffraff that you have been going around with.

GROUCHO: You mean you?

MRS. CLAYPOOL (*drawing herself up*): I mean those uncouth men that I saw you with around the opera house. I'm very grateful that they are not on board the boat.

GROUCHO: Say, I would be, too.

MRS. CLAYPOOL: I trust I shall not have to speak of this again.

GROUCHO: So do I. And that reminds me, I forgot to lock my trunk.

Shot of Harpo, Chico, and Ricardo

They are looking in at the dinner. They are in a passageway. A SHIP'S OFFICER *comes through; looks at them. They pretend elaborate unconcern. The* OFFICER *goes on his way, but unconvinced.*

Close-up—Harpo's Face, *almost in anguish.*

We Show What He Is Watching

At the table a WAITER *is serving some food to* GROUCHO.

Close-up—Chico and Ricardo Watching

CHICO: Fine friend! He come up here and eat while we starve.

RICARDO: Look! There's Rosa!

CHICO: Rosa! There's bologna—that's more like it.

Close-up—Harpo

Licking his lips as he watches.

A Shot of What He's Looking At

We see a WAITER *serving huge portion of food.*

Back to Harpo

He can hardly stand it. A little Dog is passing; he picks it up and takes a bite. The Dog yelps; he drops it, and he, Chico and Ricardo streak it away.

Shot of the Orchestra *striking up.*

Groucho, Guili, and Mrs. Claypool

Simultaneously Guili and Groucho address Mrs. Claypool.

Guili and Groucho *(together, as they rise)*: Shall we dance?

Groucho: I wasn't talking to you, Guili.

Guili: I was not talking to you. . . . Mrs. Claypool, may I have the honor.

Mrs. Claypool *(looking from one to the other)*: I really don't know what to do.

Groucho *(reaching over and treading heavily on Guili's foot)*: I'll fix that. . . . Ready, Mrs. Claypool?

Mrs. Claypool: If you will pardon me, Mr. Guili?

Guili *(concealing the injured foot)*: Certainly.

Groucho and Mrs. Claypool on the Dance Floor

Groucho: Do you rumba?

Mrs. Claypool: I certainly do.

Groucho: All right—think of a rumba from one to ten.

They continue dancing.

The Steerage Again

Music is playing gaily as the camera moves from group to group. Everyone is eating.

Harpo, Chico, and Ricardo

As they discover the steerage. Their eyes sweep the scene.

Chico: Everybody eat down here, too.

Harpo gives a whistle; points.

A Table, laden with Food

Back to Scene

CHICO: What do you think? *(HARPO nods)* All right. Let's go.
The CAMERA PANS with them as they walk over to the table, very nonchalantly. They load up their plates, piling them with all kinds of food.

Dissolve to:
The Three Boys

Eating away for dear life.

The Musicians *as their melody comes to a climax and stops. A few of the MUSICIANS leave their places.*

Harpo, Chico, Etc.

They are just finishing their food. In the background we see the MUSICIANS arrive at the food table.

CHICO: Ah, that was good. How do you feel now, Tomasso? *(HARPO gives a satisfied nod)* How about you, Ricardo? How are you?

RICARDO: Never better!

By way of proving it, he bursts into a few bars of "Ridi, Pagliacci," very gaily. HARPO dashes to the harp. CHICO runs to the piano. The three of them start to SING and PLAY. The CROWD APPLAUDS.

THE LEADER: Here, here! Stop that! Get away from there.

The MUSIC stops. The CROWD, however, immediately protests—"Aw, let 'em play!" "Yeh, let 'em play!" "Come on!" The number now formally begins. (The dance. The specialties.)

Upper Deck

LASSPARRI *and* CAPTAIN. *Suspicion.*

The Captain and the Other Officers *are trying to reach* CHICO, HARPO, *and* RICARDO. *The* DANCING PASSENGERS *render it difficult, so that at times the* CAPTAIN *and* HIS MEN *are caught up in the dance itself.*

The Three Boys *are* PLAYING *more and more furiously, at the same time looking around for a way to escape. Wherever they look, there is a group of* OFFICERS.

The DANCING *grows more and more gay, the* MUSIC *louder. Slowly but surely,* THE BOYS *are hemmed in. The* MUSIC *approaches a climax.*

Inside, Detention Cabin, *as already shot.*

The Boat from the Outside *as it rolls in the water.*

Close-up—Porthole from the Outside
The water going into the room.

Inside, the Room Again
HARPO *has been knocked down by the water.*
CHICO *(rushes over and closes the porthole)*: What you want to do? Drown us? . . . What are you eating? Where'd you get something to eat?
The CAMERA CUTS *to* HARPO; *he is happily chewing.*
CHICO: What you got? Let's see!
HARPO *brings his hand from behind his back. It seems that a fish has been washed into the room. One bite has already been taken out of it.*

Rosa's Room
ROSA *sits there, crying softly.* GROUCHO *stands beside her. The door to the room is open.*
GROUCHO: Listen—that's six handkerchiefs of mine you've ruined, and that's all I've got, so you've got to stop.

ROSA: Why didn't you tell me Ricardo was aboard? Maybe I could have done something.

GROUCHO: That's what I was afraid of. Now stop worrying.

ROSA: But they'll send him back to Italy.

GROUCHO: Well, he isn't back there yet. *(He starts to leave)* You leave everything to me. Otis B. Driftwood has never failed yet. I've been through bankruptcy twice, but I've never failed. I'll see you later.

The CAMERA FOLLOWS GROUCHO *as he goes toward his own cabin. A* MAN *in uniform is standing outside his door.*

GROUCHO: Hello. What are you doing here?

THE MAN: They think you're in with the stowaways. I've got orders to follow you.

GROUCHO: Well, you can't follow me in here because there's only room for one of us. *(*GROUCHO *goes into his room—closes the door)*

The Room Downstairs

HARPO's *fish is now a skeleton.*

CHICO: Get that thing out of here!

HARPO *opens the porthole, first trying to time his action to the lurching of the ship. He tosses out the fish, but more water comes in.*

CHICO: Close it! Close it!

HARPO *tries to close it, but can't.* CHICO *and* RICARDO *rush to help him, but the porthole sticks. At each roll of the boat more water comes in.*

CHICO: Now see what you do. We drown! *(He beats on the door)*

Outside the Door

The BEATING *is heard from inside, but the* GUARD *is impassive.*

Inside the Room Again

More water. It is up to their knees. HARPO *leans out of the porthole;* WHISTLES *shrilly for help.*

Groucho's Room

He is leaning on the porthole. HARPO's *whistle is heard.* GROUCHO *leans over and looks down the side of the boat.* HARPO's *head is a small speck, far below and considerably to one side.* GROUCHO *pulls out the field glasses; looks down and recognizes* HARPO. *He gives a* WHISTLE *in return; waves his arm. Looks around, wondering what he can do.* HARPO WHISTLES *again; points to the rope, which hangs within* GROUCHO's *reach, but not within* HARPO's. GROUCHO, *first taking the precaution of locking his door, grabs the rope and tries to swing it over so that* HARPO *can catch hold of it.*

The Room Downstairs—Shot from Outside the Boat

HARPO *repeatedly reaching for the rope, which just escapes him with each roll of the boat. Finally he gets it; gives a great* WHISTLE *of triumph.*

Inside the Lower Room

CHICO: You got it? (HARPO *nods*) You go first. If it's safe, then we come after.

HARPO *takes a firm grasp on the rope and swings out of the porthole. Just then the ship gives a terrific lurch and* HARPO *is dipped right into the ocean.*

In a moment he comes up again, as the ship rolls the other way. He brings with him a fisherman's net and the entire morning's catch. Huge crabs crawl over him; other fish are entangled with him in the net.

The Lower Porthole

CHICO *(to* RICARDO*)*: You can tell it's Friday.

Close-up—Harpo

With terrific struggles, he tries to rid himself of the net and the fish, one at a time.

Groucho's Porthole

GROUCHO: Too bad. The big one got away.

Harpo Again

*He gets rid of the final fish, then starts to climb up the rope.
He gets almost up to GROUCHO's room. GROUCHO reaches out
a hand to grasp him.*

The Top Deck

*A SAILOR is turning a windlass, to which the rope is fastened.
He lets the rope out; the handle of the windlass whirls around.*

Harpo Again

He is shot all the way down, right into the water.

Groucho's Porthole

GROUCHO: What a diver! That's the greatest dive I've seen since
General Electric went down a hundred points.

Harpo in the Ocean

*He grabs the rope and climbs up a little ways. Then he feels
something biting him. Reaches quickly into his hip pocket,
pulls out a fish and throws it furiously into the water. He starts
to climb again, but is too exhausted. He cannot go any farther.
He makes for the nearest porthole—there is a GIRL under a
shower. She screams; HARPO watches for a second in admira-
tion.*

The Sailor on the Top Deck

This time he works the windlass the other way.

Harpo Again

*He is shot rapidly up—much farther than he wants to go. From
the windlass the rope runs up some fifty feet before it is looped
through a pulley and allowed to descend. HARPO, accordingly,*

51

128028

is now forty feet above the boat. The SAILOR, *not seeing him, walks blandly away.*

Groucho's Porthole
GROUCHO *(looking up at* HARPO*)*: Well, maybe I'd better buy General Electric again.

Harpo Again
He starts to descend the rope.

Chico's Porthole
RICARDO *(to* CHICO *who is peering up)*: What's he doing now?
CHICO: I think he hang himself.

Groucho's Porthole
HARPO finally arrives outside the porthole, as GROUCHO *helps him the final few feet.*
GROUCHO: That's it . . . A little farther . . . Give me your hand . . . That's right . . . Here we are.
There is a heavy KNOCK *on the door.*
GROUCHO *(whispers to* HARPO*)*: You can't come in here—they're watching the room. You've got to find some other room. Do you understand?
HARPO nods. Swings to one side; peers into another stateroom.

Shot Through Porthole
A magnificent cabin. Three beds, side by side. The THREE AVIATORS *asleep, the black beards carefully outside the covers.*

Harpo, Outside the Porthole
He gives a reassuring nod to GROUCHO.

Groucho's Porthole
He nods back.

Inside the Aviators' Cabin

HARPO *climbs through. Looks at the sleeping forms; considers. Sees a scissors. Picks it up and approaches the* TRIO, *a smile on his face.*

Fade out

Fade in:
Ship Going Through the Harbor

Tugs and airplanes greeting it.

A Welcoming Crowd on the Dock

A Banner Stretched Across the Dock:

WELCOME TO THE HEROES OF THE AIR

A Welcoming Committee, *in high hats, coming up the gangplank.*

On the Deck

The CAPTAIN *and his* OFFICERS *appear. The* WELCOMING COMMITTEE, *consisting of some half a dozen men, come aboard and start to shake hands.*

CAPTAIN: Good morning, gentlemen! How do you do? . . . Good morning. . . . Good morning.

THE COMMITTEE: Good morning, Captain.

GROUCHO *appears.*

GROUCHO: Gentlemen, our distinguished guests have asked me to represent them and to act as their interpreter. Now if you will follow me to the cabin where I last saw them, there's at least a chance that they'll still *be* there.

Outside Suite A-B-C

GROUCHO, *the* CAPTAIN, *and the* WELCOMING COMMITTEE *appear.* GROUCHO KNOCKS *on the door; nothing happens for a second. He opens the door an inch and peeps in.*

53

Inside the Cabin

Through the crack of the door we see HARPO, CHICO, *and* RICARDO, *now dressed in the regalia of the aviators, gluing on a few final hairs of their beards.*

GROUCHO *(quickly closing the door)*: Pardon me. Our distinguished guests are—ah—chinning. They'll be right out.

The door is now opened wide. The BOYS *come out—uniforms, medals, beards, and all. The beards are none too neat, and the clothes hang none too well on* CHICO *and* HARPO.

THE COMMITTEE: Ah—gentlemen!

The BOYS *bow, not daring to risk speech.*

COMMITTEE LEADER *(producing a manuscript)*: My friends, it is with a full heart—

GROUCHO: Here—give me that. Let's cut this short. *(He looks at the manuscript)* The whole thing is very simple. They want you to go to City Hall, and the Mayor is going to make another speech. *(He tears up the manuscript)* We can tear the Mayor's speech up when we get there.

A SHIP'S OFFICER *rushes excitedly up.*

OFFICER: Captain! Captain! The stowaways have escaped!

CAPTAIN: What? Well, they couldn't get off the boat! Where *are* they?

For answer HARPO *merely opens the door of* SUITE A-B-C. *Lying on the beds, securely bound are the* THREE AVIATORS, *now clean-shaven and dressed in the clothes of* RICARDO, CHICO, *and* HARPO.

The Street

GROUCHO *and the* THREE BOYS *just taking their places in the official car. A* CAPTAIN OF POLICE *is addressing them, introducing a newcomer.*

CAPTAIN OF POLICE *(saluting)*: Gentlemen, this is Detective Sergeant Henderson, who will act as your personal bodyguard.

GROUCHO: He's not dressed like a sergeant.

CAPTAIN: He's a plain-clothes man.

GROUCHO: He looks more like an old-clothes man.

HENDERSON (*taking the seat beside the driver*): At your service, gentlemen. If there's anything I can do, don't hesitate to call on me.

GROUCHO (*as the car starts*): All right, driver. Let's call on Mr. Henderson—that's the first stop.

Broadway

The DISTINGUISHED VISITORS *riding through a confetti-swept city. Glimpses of the* CROWD, PEOPLE *in windows, etc.*

Close-up—the Automobile

HARPO *lounging back at his ease, with his feet practically on* HENDERSON's *shoulders.* HENDERSON *is none too pleased.*

City Hall Steps—the Official Reception

Microphones, a huge CROWD, *the* MAYOR *speaking. Our* FOUR BOYS *stand in a line, with* HENDERSON *beside them. A table, with water pitcher and glasses, beside the* MAYOR, *who is just finishing drinking a glass of water.*

Close Shot—of Photographers *snapping pictures of the scene.*

Back to Scene

MAYOR: And so, my friends, as Mayor of this great city, I take pleasure in inviting our distinguished visitors to tell us something of their achievements.

He motions to CHICO. APPLAUSE *from the* CROWD, *of course.*

Close-up—Chico and Groucho

CHICO (*whispering*): What'll I say?

GROUCHO: Tell 'em you're not here.

CHICO: What if they don't believe me?

GROUCHO: They'll believe you when you start speaking.

55

Back to Scene

CHICO *advances to the microphones. Takes a little sip of water before* SPEAKING.

CHICO: My friends, how we happen to come to America is a great story, if I could tell it. When we first start out, we have no idea you give us this great reception. And when I say we are not entitled to this reception, I know more about that than you do. So instead I tell you how we get these medals.

GROUCHO: If you do, I'm getting off here.

CHICO: You think we get these medals for flying. But you are wrong—the medals come with the suit. First get the suit and you have got the medals. The only question is how to get the suit. That is the whole secret of flying. And once you get in the flying machine, remember this: keep the head still, the left arm stiff *(He takes a golf stance)* and follow through.

He completes the swing, hands clenched together as though holding a club. At the completion of the swing he hits HENDERSON *squarely in the face with his two hands and knocks him down.*

GROUCHO *(bounding to the microphone)*: What a sock that was! Henderson is down! Seven, eight, nine *(*HENDERSON *is shown getting to his feet)* he's up again! What a fight, folks! I wish you were all here and I was home, listening in on another program. And now you will hear again from the Mayor, who was so dull the first time he spoke. All right, Mr. Mayor—take it away.

MAYOR: This is the Mayor again. And now I take great pleasure in introducing another of our heroes, who will tell you about some of his exploits. *(He leads* HARPO *forward—applause)*

MAYOR *(to* HARPO): I suggest that your speech should be a little more direct than your brother's.

HARPO, scared, looks the CROWD *over. Then he sees the water pitcher; pours himself a glass of water, faces the microphone again; takes a second glass of water. Once more he comes forward; then a third glass of water.*

56

We see an ATTENDANT'S *arm remove the pitcher and replace it with a full one.*

GROUCHO: We're all right as long as the water supply holds out. *(*HARPO *immediately takes a fourth glass)* I think I'll join you. *(He also takes a glass)*

CHICO: I'll take one too.

RICARDO: Make mine the same.

MAYOR *(indicating the microphone)*: Please, please!

CHICO: We got plenty of time. *(He turns to the boys)* One more round—this one is on me. *(They all drink again; another pitcher of water is set down)*

GROUCHO: Now, just one more, and then we'll *all* go home. *(They drink again)*

MAYOR: Gentlemen, gentlemen!

CHICO: What do you say—one more? Just one. *(They pour and drink again)*

MAYOR: But, gentlemen—

GROUCHO *(glass in hand; addressing the* MAYOR*)*: Say, where do you get this? This is good stuff.

Close-up—Henderson's Face, Watching Them Narrowly

Back to Scene

CHICO *(drinking)*: My wife's the greatest little woman in the world. No, I'm not married. Your wife's the greatest little woman in the world.

By this time the BOYS *are pouring and drinking, pouring and drinking.*

MAYOR: Please, gentlemen!

High hat in hand, he mops his brow. HARPO *obliges by pouring a glass of water into the hat. The* MAYOR *puts on the hat; water pours down over him. A* COMMITTEE MEMBER LAUGHS; *the* MAYOR *glares at him. The* COMMITTEE MEMBER, *straight-*

57

ening his face, hurriedly puts on his own hat, and water pours down over him.

MAYOR *(forcing a laugh, and handing the microphone to* HARPO*)*: The—the radio is waiting.

HARPO *stands for a moment before the instrument, then spouts a stream of water. It narrowly misses* CHICO *and lands on* HENDERSON, *who is furious.*

HENDERSON *advances on* HARPO, *blood in his eye. At that moment* CHICO *spurts a stream of water at* HARPO; HARPO *ducks and* HENDERSON *gets it again.*

The trick is repeated again. That is, HENDERSON *makes for* CHICO *and receives* HARPO's *next torrent. This time, however, about half of the* COMMITTEE *also gets it.*

GROUCHO: Well, it looks as if the drought is over.

CHICO *backs away and sets himself for a terrific spouting.* HARPO *again escapes, but about fifty other people get it.* HARPO *also backing away—the crowd is quite willing to clear a path—now spouts a terrific stream. A full hundred* PEOPLE *are soaked.*

Close-ups—Mayor and Henderson

Back to Scene

GROUCHO *(at the microphone)*: Well, folks, I still wish you were here. It's the greatest thing since the Johnstown flood. *(Another great stream from* HARPO, *now some fifty feet away, and not far from the Civic Virtue fountain. A bigger stream from* CHICO. *Then two streams crossing each other—a very pretty effect)* This may be the last reception ever held in New York.

Close-up—Henderson and Mayor, with Groucho Listening

HENDERSON: Listen, I'm getting suspicious of these guys. I don't think they're aviators at all.

MAYOR: Neither do I.

58

The Civic Virtue Fountain

HARPO *on the fountain, having replaced the figure of Civic Virtue. He is spouting magnificently, and in beautiful symmetric designs. Half a dozen fish emerge from his mouth.*

Groucho at the Microphone

GROUCHO: Ladies and gentlemen, this concludes the celebration. Because the distinguished aviators, if they have any sense, are now going to scram out of here.

GROUCHO *is sprinting away from the microphone on the*

Fade out

Fade in:
Close-up—Signboard Reading:

ELLIS ISLAND

Office of Commissioner of Immigration

The COMISSIONER *is seated at a huge desk. Also present are* HENDERSON, GUILI, LASSPARRI, *and the* THREE AVIATORS— *still smooth-shaven, but again in uniform. There are, perhaps, the beginnings of new beards.*

COMMISSIONER: Gentlemen, I cannot tell you how I regret this unfortunate incident. You are released with full apologies.

The AVIATORS *bow.*

HENDERSON: Now the next thing to do is to catch those three crooks and deport 'em. *(He turns to* LASSPARRI*)* And from the description you've given me I'll have 'em within twenty-four hours.

LASSPARRI: That will be very good.

GUILI *(with venom)*: If I were you I would question Mr. *Otis B. Driftwood.*

HENDERSON: You bet I will. And if he had anything to do with this, *he's* going to jail too.

59

Close-up—Newspaper Story:

IMPOSTORS PLAY HOAX ON MAYOR

Stowaways Impersonate Famous

Aviators at City Hall

Reception

APOLOGY TO REAL FLIERS

Immigration Authorities Search

for Men Throughout City

While a crowd of ten thousand cheered them to the echo on the steps of City Hall, three stowaways, posing as the world-famous aviators, received the keys of the city yesterday from the Mayor of New York. It was not until the impressive ceremony had been concluded that the gigantic hoax was discovered.

Accompanying the story is a photograph of the City Hall proceedings, taken as the MAYOR *was putting down his glass of water. Ranged in a row are* RICARDO, CHICO, *and* HARPO—*in the uniforms and beards of the* AVIATORS, *of course. A caption on this photograph reads:*

HERE ARE THE THREE STOWAWAYS WHO FOOLED

CITY HALL

The CAMERA DRAWS BACK *and reveals that the paper is held by* GROUCHO. *Wearing a bathrobe, he is seated at a breakfast table set for four. The* WAITER *is just finishing putting down the food. He goes.*

GROUCHO *(with the paper)*: Well, this simplifies everything. Up to now all I had to do was to get rid of *these* guys. Now I've got to get rid of these guys *and* the police. *(*RICARDO *comes out of the next room, tying his tie. He indulges in a little* VOCAL FLIGHT *as he enters)* What are you singing about? Did you see this? *(*RICARDO *looks)*

RICARDO *(a low* WHISTLE*)*: What are you going to do?

GROUCHO: Do? I'm going to throw those two gorillas out of here. And that goes for you too. *(The* CAMERA STARTS TO MOVE BACK *to reveal the two rooms)* I thought I got rid of those fellows when I sold my trunk.

The CAMERA, *having shown the double room for a moment, now* MOVES IN *on the bedroom. There are four beds, with* HARPO *and* CHICO *in two of them. The alarm clock* SOUNDS. HARPO *socks it with a mallet and goes back to sleep.*

CHICO *(waking up)*: I'm cold.

HARPO *puts an empty bed on top of him.*

The Living Room

GROUCHO *(ringing a bell)*: Come on, Kiddies! Kiddies!

The Bedroom

HARPO *throws the bed off; they rush into the other room.*

The Living Room

HARPO *and* CHICO *enter; go right to the food.*

GROUCHO *(handing* CHICO *the newspaper)*: Here! This'll take away your appetite.

CHICO *(takes a look, in the midst of eating)*: No, no, it just make me hungrier.

HARPO *prepares the cup cake.*

CHICO: No, I don't like cup cakes.

HARPO *and the hot dog. His reflection in the dish-cover. The make-up scene.*

GROUCHO *(to* HARPO*)*: If you're getting dressed up to get out of here, that suits me.

CHICO: No, no, we like it here. Nice beds, good food, you pay the bills.

GROUCHO: Listen, I haven't paid a hotel bill in thirty years and I'm not going to start now. Now, why don't you boys be nice? Get out of here before I get arrested.

CHICO: No, I'd like to stay and see it.

There is a sharp KNOCK *on the door.*

RICARDO (*as he,* HARPO, *and* CHICO *all look up with some alarm*): Who's that?

Another KNOCK. CHICO *goes to the door.*

CHICO: If it's a policeman, knock once more. (*Another* KNOCK) That'sa good enough for me. Come on, boys.

CHICO, RICARDO, *and* HARPO *are seen going through the window, onto the fire escape, which extends along the outside of the bedroom window and the living-room window.*

GROUCHO *now opens the door. It is* HENDERSON *who stands outside.*

GROUCHO (*in the tone of one greeting an utter stranger*): Yes?

HENDERSON: You remember me. (*He is entering the room*) I'm Henderson.

GROUCHO: Oh, yes. You're from the exterminator company. All right—just give me a once-over. (*He sits down*)

HENDERSON (*picking up the newspaper*): Interesting story in the morning paper—isn't it?

GROUCHO: Yes. Isn't it? Nice photograph, too.

HENDERSON (*too, too agreeably*): *Very* nice. . . . You live here all alone, do you?

GROUCHO: Yes. I'm practically a hermit.

HENDERSON: Um-hum. (*He eyes the breakfast table*) I—ah—I notice the table is set for four.

GROUCHO: That's nothing. My alarm clock is set for eight. That doesn't prove anything.

HENDERSON *strolls over and looks into the bedroom. He walks in as we see* GROUCHO *looking worried in the other room.* HENDERSON, *in the bedroom, surveys the mussed bed and the Army cots.*

HENDERSON (*calling to* GROUCHO): Hey, you! (GROUCHO *scurries in*) What is a hermit doing with four beds?

GROUCHO: Well, I'll tell you. You see those first three beds? I counted five thousand sheep in those three beds last night. So I had to have another bed to sleep in—you wouldn't want me to sleep with the sheep, would you?

HENDERSON *peers into the bathroom; the shower curtains are drawn.* HENDERSON *pulls them open.*

GROUCHO: Well, I fooled you that time—I only use one shower.

HENDERSON *draws the curtains shut; strolls back through the bedroom; peers under the beds. Meanwhile* GROUCHO *has strolled over to the window of the living room; peers out, looking toward the left.*

We See Chico and Harpo *in a spot between the two windows, and* RICARDO *farther over, squeezed against the building.*

Close-up—Casino Game
A six and an ace are lying on the board.

Back to:
Groucho
GROUCHO *(to* HARPO*)*: You've got a seven—take 'em.

Harpo *looks up; nods his thanks and takes the trick.*

Living Room
HENDERSON *comes out of the bedroom just at this moment.*
HENDERSON: What did you say?
GROUCHO: Me? I didn't say a word.
HENDERSON *(strolls to window)*: I heard somebody say something. . . . Ah! What's this? *(He peers out—straight out, so that he does not see the* BOYS*)*
GROUCHO: That's a fire escape and this is a room and there's the door. And I wish—*(leaning against wall posed* à la *Garbo)*—I wish you'd go. I want to be alone.
HENDERSON: You'll be alone as soon as I get the evidence.
He steps out on fire escape. As he does so CHICO *and* HARPO *step from fire escape into bedroom, and resume playing their game on one of the cots.*

63

Henderson on the Fire Escape, *looking around.* RICARDO *is now squeezed into a little ledge, so that* HENDERSON *does not see him.* HENDERSON *proceeds to the bedroom window.*

Inside the Bedroom HARPO *and* CHICO *hear* HENDERSON, *stop playing, lift up the cot and carry it through to the living room.*
GROUCHO: When he gets out of here, we'll make it three-handed.

Henderson Stepping into the Bedroom Window
As he does so HARPO *and* CHICO *step out of the living-room window.* HENDERSON *looks around and sees that a cot is missing.*
HENDERSON *(to* GROUCHO*)*: Hey, you!
GROUCHO *(scurrying in again)*: Coming—
HENDERSON: What became of that fourth bed?
GROUCHO: Why, I don't know what you mean.
HENDERSON: The last time I was in this room there were four beds here!
GROUCHO: Sounds like an orgy. I'm not interested in your private life, Henderson.
HENDERSON: Bah! *(He steps into the living room, closely followed by* GROUCHO. *He stops in amazement as he sees the cot)* Say, what's this bed doing here?
GROUCHO *(scrutinizing bed carefully)*: I don't see it doing anything.
At this point HARPO *and* CHICO *re-enter the bedroom and resume their game on another cot.*
HENDERSON: There's something mighty funny going on around here.
GROUCHO: Not in this scene there isn't.
HENDERSON *goes on fire escape again.* BOYS *enter living room with second cot.*
GROUCHO: Who's ahead?
CHICO: You owe us a dollar apiece.
HENDERSON *comes in the bedroom again, which is cue for*

64

BOYS *to exit by fire escape.* HENDERSON *surveys scene and again* CALLS.

HENDERSON: Hey, you!

GROUCHO *(rushing into bedroom)*: Coming!

HENDERSON: Am I crazy or are there only two beds here?

GROUCHO: Which question do you want me to answer first?

HENDERSON *(rushing into living room and spying the two cots there)*: Ah! How did those two beds get together?

GROUCHO: Well, you know how those things are—they breed like rabbits.

By this time HARPO *and* CHICO *have re-entered the bedroom.* HARPO *turns cot on end, sticks his fist through the opening in the center and stands back of the closed door. He opens door and cot fits into doorway.*

HENDERSON *(to* GROUCHO*)*: I'll solve this, if I have to stay here all night!

He grabs what he thinks is the doorknob, but is HARPO'*s fist, turns it, and walks into the bedroom as* HARPO *calmly walks into the living room, where* GROUCHO *helps him arrange the cots.* HENDERSON *sees that only the bed remains and flutters around* CALLING *frantically.*

HENDERSON: One bed—

He goes to the fire escape, at which point CHICO *comes out of the bathroom and with* GROUCHO'*s assistance, puts the fourth bed into the living room while* HARPO *puts the breakfast table and chairs into the bedroom.* GROUCHO *sits down at the breakfast table and* CHICO *and* HARPO *rush into the bathroom. As* HENDERSON *reappears at the fire escape, at the living-room window, he comes in and finds that the living room is apparently the bedroom.*

HENDERSON: Maybe I *am* crazy!

He rushes into the bedroom, where GROUCHO *is calmly drinking coffee. With a* SCREAM, HENDERSON *runs to the fire escape.*

GROUCHO: Well, now I can take my shower.

As he starts for the bedroom he is peeling off his bathrobe;

he wears pajamas underneath. He arrives at the bathroom; opens the shower curtains. HARPO *and* CHICO *are sitting on the floor of the tub, apparently stripped and with the water pouring down over them. They are still playing casino, slapping the cards down on the floor of the tub.*

GROUCHO *(as he starts to disrobe)*: All right—deal me in.

Henderson on the Fire Escape

He descends one flight, looking around. One or two flights farther down is RICARDO, *hanging onto a window ledge. As* HENDERSON's *feet near him he* JUMPS *into the room as his only method of escape.*

Inside, Another Room

It is empty. RICARDO *looks around—it is a bedroom and obviously a woman's. It turns out—surprise, surprise!—to be* ROSA's *room. Immediately, she enters. As the door opens* RICARDO *shrinks back; then quickly sees who it is.*

ROSA: Ricardo!

RICARDO: Rosa! *(They rush into each other's arms)* So! You thought you could come to America without me, eh?

ROSA: Oh, you fool! You dear, dear fool!

RICARDO: Because I'm in love with you, you call me a fool. Well, maybe there's something *in* that. *(He kisses her)*

ROSA: You know, if you were going to stow away on that boat you might at least have told me about it.

RICARDO: Well, the whole thing came up pretty suddenly. I didn't even have time to pack—I had to use another man's trunk.

ROSA: But what are you doing *here*?

RICARDO: Easiest thing in the world. An open window, a detective, and here I am.

ROSA: Ricardo, you *shouldn't* have. They'll only send you back again—perhaps even put you in jail.

RICARDO: I don't care. It's worth it.

ROSA: Suppose I went to Mr. Guili—maybe he'd intercede for you.

RICARDO: Guili wouldn't do anything—Lassparri's got to him first.

ROSA: But there must be *something* we can do. *(A* KNOCK *on the door)*

ROSA *(points to closet)*: Get in there! *(He does so)* Who is it? *(The door opens and* LASSPARRI *enters)* Why, Rudolfo!

LASSPARRI: You do not mind my dropping in?

ROSA: No—of course not. Only—I was just going to take a nap.

LASSPARRI: Rosa, why do you do this to me?

ROSA: Do what, Rudolfo?

LASSPARRI: Whenever I want to see you, you make some excuse. You will not dine with me; you will not ride with me; you won't even take a walk with me.

ROSA: But Rudolfo, you know how busy I am—my debut in America.

LASSPARRI: Well, have you forgotten that it was I who brought about your debut in America? *(He puts an arm around her)*

ROSA *(side-stepping)*: No—of course I haven't forgotten.

LASSPARRI: Then—why do you treat me this way? *(His arm going around her again)*

ROSA *(realizing that she must face the situation)*: Rudolfo, I must ask you to leave.

LASSPARRI: Now, my dear, why not be sensible?

RICARDO *emerges from his hiding place.*

RICARDO: If you ask me, I think she's being very sensible.

LASSPARRI *(taking in the situation)*: Baroni! Well, now I understand. *(To* ROSA*)* You did not tell me you had a previous engagement.

RICARDO: Well, now you know it.

LASSPARRI: Then I must apologize. And now permit me to withdraw. In a boudoir two are company, three a crowd.

RICARDO: And just what do you mean by that?

ROSA: Ricardo, please!

LASSPARRI: Surely I have made my meaning clear. Permit me to congratulate you on your taste.

For answer RICARDO *knocks him down.*

ROSA: Ricardo, you shouldn't have done that.

LASSPARRI *is getting to his feet.*

LASSPARRI *(slowly; threateningly)*: You have not heard the end of this!

ROSA *(not caring)*: I'm sure I haven't.

LASSPARRI: You may be *very sure.*

He looks at her for a second; then goes.

ROSA: Ricardo, you must go. He'll tell the police.

RICARDO *scoots to the fire escape; puts one leg through.*

RICARDO *(turning)*: I won't go till I get one more kiss.

She goes over and kisses him. He leaves.

Fade out

Close-up—Two or Three Hands, Apparently Hammering
Underneath the scene is the Anvil Chorus, and the various hands are descending on the beat.

Camera Draws Farther Back, *and shows the bare stage of the opera house, with the* ENSEMBLE *in rehearsal. The music stops suddenly as a distracted* CONDUCTOR RAPS *for order. Surrounding him in the pit are the* MUSICIANS, *in shirt sleeves. Handkerchiefs in their collars, etc.*

CONDUCTOR: No, no, no, no, no, no! Now listen to me. Tonight we are opening! We open the season with the great Lassparri and you sing like that! Now! Once more, and I want to hear it! *(He gives the signal; the singing begins again)*

Outside the Stage Door
The STAGE DOORMAN *is present.*

GROUCHO *comes along. Spats, a cane, very gay.* SINGING.

GROUCHO: Afternoon, Tim!

DOORMAN *(very obsequious)*: Good afternoon, Mr. Driftwood. Ready for the opening tonight?

GROUCHO: Certainly am. Listen to this. *(He indulges in a fancy* VOCAL FLIGHT *as he passes into the opera house)*

CAMERA FOLLOWS HIM *backstage. The card game. When he reaches there, the* THREE STAGEHANDS *leap respectfully to their feet. Give a little gesture of greeting.*

GROUCHO: That's all right, boys—I was young myself once. *(He glances toward the stage, greeting the* BOYS *and* GIRLS*)* Hello! Hello! *(The* CONDUCTOR *stops the music, bows. There is a respectful chorus of* "How do you do, Mr. Driftwood?" "How do you do?")

The CAMERA *again* FOLLOWS GROUCHO *to the elevator. A waiting* ELEVATOR MAN *is all bows and smiles.*

ELEVATOR MAN: Waiting for you, Mr. Driftwood. Step right in.

GROUCHO: Thank you, Herman. *(The door is closing, the elevator starting)*

HERMAN *(heard and seen through the gratings as the car rises)*: Nice day today, isn't it?

Upstairs—the Elevator Arriving

GROUCHO *steps out.*

GROUCHO: Thank you, Herman.

Immediately opposite is a door lettered:

OTIS B. DRIF

A MAN *is busily scraping the name off.* HERMAN, *in open elevator door, waits and watches.*

GROUCHO: What's all this? What's going on here?

THE MAN: You mean, what's coming off here.

GROUCHO: But you can't do that.

THE MAN *(wiping another letter off)*: Want to bet?

GROUCHO: But that's my office.

THE MAN: I got my orders from Mr. Guili. Take it up with him.

GROUCHO *stalks down the corridor to* GUILI's *office.*

Close-up—Door

ARTURO GUILI
Director-General

GROUCHO *opens the door—goes in.*

69

Guili's Office as Groucho Enters

Present are GUILI, LASSPARRI, HENDERSON, *and* MRS. CLAY-POOL.

GROUCHO: What's the meaning of this? If you think——

Close-ups—the Four Faces, Sternly Regarding Him

The first face is that of HENDERSON, *which brings* GROUCHO *up with a start.*

GROUCHO *(changing his mind about the whole thing)*: Well, if you're busy I'll come in again. *(He starts out)*

GUILI: One minute, Mr. Driftwood. We have some news for you.

GROUCHO: News? For me?

GUILI: Mrs. Claypool has decided to dispense with your services immediately.

GROUCHO: Dispense with my services? Why, she hasn't had 'em.

MRS. CLAYPOOL: I warned you, Mr. Driftwood, that if you continued to associate with those men, everything would be over between us.

HENDERSON *(hard as nails)*: And you've been associating with them.

GROUCHO: How do *you* know? *You* couldn't find them.

HENDERSON: Those men will be under arrest within twenty-four hours.

GROUCHO: Oh, that means you're off the case.

HENDERSON: And when I get *them* I'm going to arrest *you* as an accomplice.

MRS. CLAYPOOL: You have disgraced *me* and the entire opera.

GUILI: So, as Mrs. Claypool's new business manager, I must request you to get out. And stay out.

GROUCHO: Just a minute, just a minute. You can't fire me without two weeks salary. That's in Section 10 of my contract.

GUILI: I find that you have overdrawn your salary for the next six months.

HENDERSON: And there's a couple of thousand dollars missing besides that.

GROUCHO: Well, in that case I'll take *one* week's salary.

GUILI: You will take nothing. Get out.

GROUCHO: Well, if that's your best offer I'll get out. But I'm not making a nickel on it. And as for you, Mrs. Claypool, I withdraw my offer of marriage.

He stalks out with dignity, tripping over the ladder of the DOOR PAINTER. *He looks up at the door. There is nothing but an "O" left.*

GROUCHO: Well, unless you take that zero off it's still my office.

He picks himself up and proceeds to the elevator, the door of which is still standing open.

HERMAN *(in the open doorway)*: This car is for officials. Take the stairs.

GROUCHO, *at the head of the stairs, stands looking down.*

Shot of Stairs, *going down about four flights.*

Back to Groucho

GROUCHO: I can't walk all that distance.

HERMAN: All right, I'll help you.

He gives him a kick. GROUCHO *tumbles down the four flights, rolling over and over. Reaching the street level, he falls right out the stage door, into the middle of the street, and down an open manhole.*

Wipe to:

Guili's Office

GUILI *and* LASSPARRI *present.*

GUILI: But why don't you want Rosa? I brought her over here on your account.

LASSPARRI *(evasively)*: Well, I have changed my mind. This other girl—I think she is more the type.

GUILI *(with meaning)*: More the type *off* stage, perhaps.

LASSPARRI: In a way, yes.

71

GUILI: But is this other girl ready? Could she go on tonight?

LASSPARRI: I have rehearsed her perfectly.

GUILI *looks at him for a second, then takes up the telephone.*

GUILI *(into the phone)*: Get me Miss Castaldi, please.

A Bench in Bryant Park

*On it sit four disconsolate figures—*HARPO, RICARDO, CHICO, GROUCHO. *It is a bench that was built for only three, and the two end men,* HARPO *and* GROUCHO, *have none too much room.* HARPO, *finding himself slipping, braces his foot against a rock and holds his place. Finding this successful, he helps himself to a little more room.* GROUCHO, *as a result, is pushed right off of his end, and finds himself sitting on the ground.*

GROUCHO *(on the ground)*: Well, that's all I needed. I'm certainly glad I met you boys. First you get me kicked out of my job, then you get me thrown out of my hotel, and finally you push me off a park bench. Well, there's one consolation—nothing more can happen to me.

A POLICEMAN *(prodding him)*: Hey, you! Get off the grass.

GROUCHO *(getting up)*: Well, I was wrong.

CHICO: The whole thing was your fault. If you hadn't come to Italy we never would have met you, and if you hadn't come *back* from Italy we never would have been in your trunk.

GROUCHO: Yes, sir, I've certainly done well since I met you. The day you boys came into my life I had a good job and was going to marry a rich widow. Now I can't even sit on the grass.

CHICO: I'd give you my seat, but I'm sitting here.

GROUCHO: Well, that's an offer. I tell you what—I'd like to think it over for a couple of days. Where can I find you?

CHICO: Wherever you are.

GROUCHO: No, I'm sick of that. Can't we meet somewhere else?

HARPO, WHISTLING *excitedly, gets up and starts to run away.*

RICARDO *(looking after him)*: It's Rosa!

CHICO *(also leaping up)*: Rosa!

CHICO *and* RICARDO *also run out of the scene.*

GROUCHO (*lying on the bench*): Well, now I can have my bench back.

A Few Feet Away
    ROSA, RICARDO, CHICO *and* HARPO.
RICARDO: But Rosa, they couldn't do that to you.
CHICO: That Lassparri! What we do to him!
    HARPO *scurries away. The* CAMERA FOLLOWS HIM *back to the bench. He* WHISTLES *shrilly at* GROUCHO, *indicates the other group, runs part way back again, returns, pulls* GROUCHO *over.*
GROUCHO: What's the matter?
CHICO (*to* GROUCHO, *as he arrives there*): What do you think? She no sing tonight. Lassparri get Rosa fired.
    ROSA *bursts into tears.*
RICARDO: It's all my fault. If I hadn't hit Lassparri this never would have happened.
CHICO: You didn't hit him hard enough.
    Fresh tears from ROSA.
RICARDO: Don't cry, darling. We'll do something about it.
GROUCHO: And let's not waste any time. The first thing to do is go back and sit on that bench.
    They start toward the bench, but before they can get there FOUR BUMS *come along and occupy it.*
GROUCHO: Well, we've got to think of something else.

Fade out

Fade in:
Long Shot—New York Opera House
    A shot of dusk, if it is possible to get one. The building is gray and hulking. Suddenly, the lights appear in every window and the marquee shines its announcement.
    The CAMERA TRUCKS UP TO THE MARQUEE. *In electric lights thereon flashes the announcement:*
        TONIGHT—RUDOLFO LASSPARRI IN
        "IL TROVATORE"

Carriage Entrance, Opera House

There is a crush of approaching limousines—in all of them fashionably attired MEN *and* WOMEN—*waiting to pull up to the curbing and discharge the* OPERAGOERS. *Silk and opera hats everywhere in evidence.* POLICEMEN *directing the traffic jam.* FOOTMEN *and* DOORMEN *opening the doors of the motors, helping the* OCCUPANTS *dismount, giving carriage checks to the* CHAUFFEURS.

Outside the Stage Door

GUILI *enters, in tails and cape.*

Inside the Stage Door

The DOORMAN *sorting telegrams, as* GUILI *enters.*

DOORMAN: Plenty for you tonight, Mr. Guili. *(He hands him a bunch of telegrams)*

GUILI: Thank you, Tim.

Rosa's Dressing Room

ROSA *and her maid,* MARIE. *The* MAID *sits weeping while* ROSA, *in street clothes, is doing the packing.*

MARIE: It is an outrage, Miss Rosa—an outrage.

ROSA: Fortunes of war, Marie. Come on—no more weeping.
With this she picks up the costume that she has been intending to wear that night. It is too much for her. She bursts into tears. The MAID *comforts her.*

Outside Guili's Office

GUILI, *humming, opens the door with a key.*

Inside Guili's Office

As GUILI *enters.* GUILI *turns on the light. Around* GUILI's *desk, mildly to his surprise, sit* GROUCHO, RICARDO, HARPO, *and* CHICO. GUILI's *liquor and cigars are spread over the desk,*

*and all four of them have apparently been having a very good
time indeed.*

GUILI *(stunned)*: What does this mean?

GROUCHO: Ah, just the man I want to see. Guili, these are the
worst cigars I ever smoked.

CHICO: The drinks no good too. Are they? *(He turning to* HARPO*)*
  HARPO *shrugs his shoulders and drains a bottle.*

GUILI: Get out of here! All of you! I shall send for the police!

GROUCHO: Just a minute, Guili. I'll tell you what we came for.

CHICO: We make bargain with you. You let Rosa sing, we give
ourselves up. Go back to Italy.

GUILI: Oh, so you're willing to give yourselves up, are you?

CHICO: If you let Rosa sing.

GUILI: Well, I am the director of the opera company, and Rosa
does not sing. But the rest of your proposition—giving yourselves
up—that rather appeals to me. *(He takes up the phone)* Get me
Police Headquarters. Sergeant Henderson. *(*HARPO *knocks him out
with a blackjack)*

GROUCHO: Well, we'll have to talk it over with him some other
time.

RICARDO: What'll we do with him?

  HARPO *opens the door of a closet;* WHISTLES. RICARDO *starts to
  drag* GUILI *into the closet.*

CHICO: Now what about Lassparri?

RICARDO *(dropping* GUILI*)*: I'll kill him!

GROUCHO: Listen—we're not going to kill anybody till we see our
lawyer. Ricardo, you go down and take care of Rosa.

CHICO: And we take care of the opera. Eh, Tomasso? *(An eager
nod from* HARPO*)* You bet we will. We make Lassparri sorry he
ever came over here.

GROUCHO: And I'll tell you what *I'm* going to do.

RICARDO: What?

GROUCHO *(starting to take off his clothes, his eyes on* GUILI*)*: I'm
going to get dressed for the opera.

The Waiting Audience

Mrs. Claypool Sitting in Her Box

An USHER *pushes open the curtains.* GROUCHO *enters, resplendent in* GUILI's *evening clothes, cape included. They fit* GROUCHO *perfectly.*

GROUCHO: Hello, Toots!

MRS. CLAYPOOL *(outraged)*: What are *you* doing here? This is Mr. Guili's box.

GROUCHO: He couldn't come, so he gave me his ticket. And he couldn't get dressed, so he gave me his clothes.

MRS. CLAYPOOL: WHAT?

The STAGE MANAGER *appears excitedly at the box.*

STAGE MANAGER: Have you seen Mr. Guili?

MRS. CLAYPOOL: Why, no. Isn't he backstage?

STAGE MANAGER: He's disappeared. We can't find him anywhere.

GROUCHO: You didn't look in the right place.

STAGE MANAGER: But the speech! He was to make a speech before the curtain went up!

MRS. CLAYPOOL: Oh, dear! What'll we do?

A CHORD *in the orchestra; a spotlight on the box.*

STAGE MANAGER: That's it! *(To* MRS. CLAYPOOL*)* Say something!

MRS. CLAYPOOL: But I've never made a speech in my life.

GROUCHO: I'll take care of it. *(He rises)* Ladies and gentlemen—

Shot of Puzzled Audience

Back to Groucho

GROUCHO: I guess that takes in most of you. This is the opening of a new opera season—a season which has been made possible by the generous checks of—*(Turning to* MRS. CLAYPOOL *with a flourish)*—Mrs. Claypool.

The Applauding Audience

Mrs. Claypool Bowing

Back to Groucho

GROUCHO: When the curtain rises I am sure the familiar strains of Verdi's music will come back to you tonight, and Mrs. Claypool's checks will probably come back in the morning.

Gottlieb* Returning to Consciousness

Back to Groucho

GROUCHO: Tonight marks the American debut of Rudolfo Lassparri. Signor Lassparri comes from a very famous family. His mother was a well-known bass singer, and his father was the first man to stuff spaghetti with bicarbonate of soda, thus causing and curing indigestion at the same time.

Gottlieb in His Office

   Emerging from the closet, he dashes to the telephone.
GOTTLIEB: Get me Police Headquarters!

Back to Groucho

GROUCHO: And by way of welcoming Signor Lassparri, we are adding to the orchestra, for tonight only, two of the greatest musicians that ever lived. They are two men who have given their lives to music—in fact, I may say that these men are to music what Professor Einstein is to crap-shooting. . . . Signor Fiorello and Signor Tomasso.

Harpo and Chico Enter the Orchestra Pit, *dressed as musicians.*
   They bow.

The Applauding Audience

* GUILI now becomes GOTTLIEB.

The Orchestra Conductor, *puzzled, glances at* GROUCHO, *but feels compelled to accept the situation.*

Back to Groucho
GROUCHO: And now—on with the opera! Let joy be unconfined; let there be dancing in the streets, drinking in the saloons, and necking in the parlor. All right, Signor Baravelli! *(He sits down)*

The Orchestra Conductor Smiles in Response

The Audience Applauding

Orchestra Conductor Acknowledging the Applause

Gottlieb's Office
GOTTLIEB *(at the telephone)*: All right, Mr. Henderson. I will expect you in five minutes. And bring plenty of men.
He hangs up; becomes conscious of his attire; looks around for his clothes. He finds only GROUCHO's *discarded outfit. Picks it up somewhat gingerly; there is no choice but to put it on. He starts to do so, reluctantly.*

Close-ups—Harpo and Chico
CHICO *pulls a pile of sheet music from under his coat.* HARPO *inserts the sheets in the music already on the racks of the various players.*

**We Get a Close-up—the Score of the Evening,
Clearly Marked** "IL TROVATORE."
This is followed by:

Close-ups—the Music Scores That Harpo Is Inserting
They are "Take Me Out to the Ball Game," and "Waltz Me Around Again Willie."

78

The Orchestra Conductor *raises his arms, knocks with baton for order.*

The Box

GROUCHO *(to* MRS. CLAYPOOL*)*: It's none of my business, but I think there's a woodpecker in that orchestra.

The enraged face of GOTTLIEB *appears between the curtains of the box.*

GOTTLIEB: So! This is where you are!

GROUCHO *(bounding into the next box)*: You mean that's where I *was*!

The Next Box *as* GROUCHO *passes through it, bound for still other boxes. A* GENTLEMAN *has an opera hat in his lap;* GROUCHO'S *foot crushes it as he passes.*

Back to Gottlieb, Claypool Box

MRS. CLAYPOOL *(seeing* GOTTLIEB'S *costume)*: Mr. Gottlieb, what's *happened* to you?

GOTTLIEB *(as he starts to pursue* GROUCHO *into the next box)*: That Schweinhund!

He steps into the next box, but is immediately pushed back by the MAN *on whose hat the escaping* GROUCHO *had stepped.* GOTTLIEB *almost lands on the floor.*

At that moment comes the SOUND *of a very sour note on a trombone.* GOTTLIEB'S *attention is immediately caught. He looks.*

Harpo with Trombone

Quite oblivious, he is adjusting the instrument.

Orchestra Conductor Glaring at Harpo

Gottlieb Glaring at Harpo

His eyes fairly stand out from his head as he recognizes him.

GOTTLIEB *(to* MRS. CLAYPOOL, *hardly able to restrain himself)*:

79

What are you doing to me, Mrs. Claypool? These people of yours! *(He lowers his voice to a whisper, hoping that it will carry to the orchestra pit)* Baravelli!

Harpo and Trombone
He gives a tentative blow—various objects come out of the trombone. Tennis balls, balloons, etc. CHICO *takes a gun and shoots at the balloons. They burst in the air.*

Back to Gottlieb
GOTTLIEB: I am ruined! Ruined!
He dashes out of the box.

Orchestra Conductor, *glaring at* HARPO. *He knocks again for order; raises his arms once more. A moment of silence; then he gives the signal. The entire orchestra at once goes into "Take Me Out to the Ball Game." At the end of a single phrase the* CONDUCTOR KNOCKS *furiously for order; the various* PLAYERS *peer unbelievingly at their music.*

Gottlieb *running to get backstage. Holds his head in his hands as the wrong music is* PLAYED.

Groucho, in the Balcony
He is sitting right in the front row, next to a MAN *with an ear trumpet.*
GROUCHO: You know, I think I heard this opera before. At the World's Series.
DEAF MAN: Eh? What's that?
GROUCHO *(takes the ear trumpet and tosses it away)*: Give me that. Now you can enjoy the opera.

The Orchestra Pit Again
The CONDUCTOR *raising his arms, as before. The signal. The*

overture now begins. It continues for about ten seconds; then the orchestra goes into "I'm Just Wild About Harry."

Close-up—Harpo
Happily playing the jazz tune as the rest of the orchestra stops.

The Audience *reacting.*

Gottlieb Backstage
Peeping out between curtain and proscenium, trying frantically to attract the CONDUCTOR's attention. Behind him are massed a veritable battalion of STAGE MANAGERS and ASSISTANTS.

Orchestra Conductor
Misunderstanding GOTTLIEB's gesticulations; gesticulates right back at him.

Harpo
HARPO, *still PLAYING, deftly spears the high hat of an ARRIVING PATRON. Gets it just on the beat; PLAYS a single note with the hat held over the trombone, and restores the hat to the owner.*

Groucho with the Standees
GROUCHO: That'll be a lesson to that fellow to check his hat.

Gottlieb in the Corner of the Curtain, *practically expiring.*

Orchestra Conductor RAPS *again for silence; the overture resumes where it had left off.*

Harpo Again
There is a little moment of CLARINET SOLO, during which HARPO takes out a jew's harp and STRUMS an accompaniment.

81

There is then a bit of DUET *between* CHICO *and* HARPO, *which develops into something of a* MUSICAL DUEL.

Groucho Again

This time he is in the top gallery, sitting atop an EXIT *sign.*
GROUCHO *(right to the* CAMERA*)*: You know, if opera wasn't dead already, two fellows like that could kill it.

Gottlieb—Still Behind the Curtain

Presses his hands to his head; makes more signs at the CONDUCTOR.
STAGE MANAGER: Shall I stop them? What'll we do?
GOTTLIEB: No, no! The performance will go on! Ring up the curtain! I'll take care of *them*! *(He rushes away)*

The Orchestra Again

The overture mounts to a rousing climax; ends on a resounding note—but that doesn't stop CHICO *and* HARPO. *They continue to* PLAY, *more strenuously than ever.* CHICO POUNDS *the piano with everything at his command;* HARPO *pulls the sliding piece right out of the trombone; throws the trombone away, and takes the next man's violin. He saws it in half with one mighty stroke, and gives his attention to the drums. The* CONDUCTOR *is trying frantically to hush them; signals to his* MEN *to do something about it. The* MEN *respond nobly—they grab* CHICO *and* HARPO *and throw them right out of the orchestra pit, underneath the stage.*

Entrance of Lassparri

Audience Applauding

The Stage

LASSPARRI *comes down to the footlights and gets all set for the*

82

first note. *A moment of complete silence, then the orchestra starts. But what it starts is "You're the Top."*

Close-up—Orchestra Tearing Up the Music Sheets *as* CHICO *feigns innocence.*

Lassparri Again *as he goes into the real aria.*

The Box
GROUCHO: If you ask me, they tore up the wrong music.

Chico
> *As conductor, he brings up the orchestra too loud while* LASS-PARRI *is singing; indulges in argument with* PIANO PLAYER, *etc.*

Anvil Chorus
> HARPO *cracking nuts as anvil descends.*

Henderson Watching from Rear of Theater

Sparks from the Fire *going up into the air.*

Roof Over the Stage
> *Sparks get between the rotten boards. The boards begin slowly to kindle.*

Henderson Watching, *now suspicious.*

Groucho Sees Henderson *and notes his suspicion.*
> *We see* GROUCHO *leave the box.*

Henderson Again, *now convinced, he starts backstage.*

Groucho in the Wings
> *To the tune of the Anvil Chorus,* GROUCHO *gives instructions to* CHICO *and* HARPO.

83

GROUCHO: Scram, scram, out of here, because I've just seen Henderson, Henderson.

Chico in the Pit SINGS *to the music.*
CHICO: I get you. I get you. (*To the* FIRST VIOLINIST, *still* SING-ING*) Here! Here! Taka this, for I have got to leave you, leave you. (*He disappears from the pit*)

Henderson, *passes through the little door that separates the stage from auditorium.*

Groucho, Chico, and Harpo—Backstage
GROUCHO (*indicating a small section of balcony, left over from the preceding scene*): In here. (*They climb in*)

Henderson Again, *crossing backstage, looking for the* BOYS. *He is approaching the balcony piece; in another second he will find them. Just then a* NOISE *behind him turns him the other way for a second, and in that instant, a voice calls out "Okay on Number Six, Bill!" The balcony piece is suddenly hauled aloft, with the* THREE BOYS *in it.*

The Balcony as It Goes Up
GROUCHO: Men's furnishings, please.

Henderson Again, *crossing the spot where the balcony had stood, and still searching.*

The Boys Again
The balcony is right up against the roof, so close that they cannot even stand erect.
GROUCHO: Say, mighty pretty country around here.
CHICO *peers down.*

Shot from Overhead *showing* HENDERSON *walking around, two hundred feet below.*

The Boys Again

CHICO: Who's that down there?

GROUCHO: His name is Henderson. Like to meet him?

CHICO: No, that's why I came up here.

> *As* GROUCHO *and* CHICO *continue to look down,* HARPO *looks up. Sniffs a little; pulls a loose board a few inches, and discovers a raging furnace within. Brings a bag of marshmallows out of his pocket, breaks a splinter off the roof board, sticks the marshmallows onto it, and sticks them into the fire.*

Shot From Overhead

> *The opera proceeding.*

The Boys Again

GROUCHO: These are the best seats in the house—you can hardly hear anything.

> HARPO *brings the toasted marshmallows down from the fire; offers one to each.*

CHICO: Where you get these: It's hot. (HARPO *indicates the roof*) What's up there? (HARPO *pulls the board down and shows the fire raging inside*) It's a fire.

GROUCHO (*also looks*): So it is. Well, boys, we've got a nice problem. Do you want to go down there and get arrested or stay up here and get burned?

> *A section of the roof, about twenty feet long, caves right in and falls to the stage, revealing the blazing fire underneath.*

Rear of the Stage *as the burning boards fall. They land against the rear wall, far back of the stage set, and cannot be seen by the audience. Instantly, there is excitement among the* STAGE CREW.

85

A STAGEHAND: Turn in an alarm, quick!

HENDERSON: Okay! Don't let 'em stop singing or there'll be a panic. *(He dashes out)*

The Three Boys Again

A rope, representing safety, is hanging about eight feet away. They cannot reach it. Finally HARPO *stands on the edge of the balcony, his feet firmly clasped by* GROUCHO *and* CHICO. *Keeping his body rigid, he bends forward as far as possible. He just misses the rope, and in so doing almost falls, at the same time nearly pulling the other two to the floor. He tries again, but it is just an inch beyond his grip. He blows, to start the rope swinging. Reverses the process, inhaling heavily as the rope swings toward him. By this trick he finally gets it.*

Backstage

STAGEHANDS *are clearing away burning boards. Another* MAN *working with a fire extinguisher. . . . Constantly, of course, against the* MUSIC *of the opera.*

The Three Boys Again, *all three descending by rope, but still high up. Then comes a* HIGH NOTE *from a* SOPRANO—*the* BOYS *quickly scamper up a few feet. Rather the fire than the* SOPRANO.

Rosa's Dressing Room

ROSA *and* RICARDO *rushing out of the room.*

RICARDO: Something's the matter!

The Boys Descending the Rope

HARPO, *farthest down, suddenly comes to the end of the rope, about fifty feet from the ground.* HARPO WHISTLES *a warning to the boys.*

GROUCHO: Well, we've reached the end of our rope.

Backstage, Just Below the Rope

RICARDO *and* ROSA *are just arriving there—*HARPO WHISTLES *to attract their attention.*

ROSA: Ricardo! Look!

RICARDO: Hang on! I can reach you!

ROSA: Ricardo! Be careful!

RICARDO *rushes for the stairs. He must ascend four flights, and the steps are half afire as he dashes up them.*

On Stage

The opera in progress—now having reached the convent scene, Act 2, Scene 2.

While LOUISA *or the* COUNT *is singing,* LASSPARRI *begins to smell smoke. He is uneasy.*

A Smoky Corridor, Lined with Dressing Rooms

RICARDO *gropes his way through,* KNOCKING *on doors and throwing them open.* GIRLS *in various stages of attire pour out of the rooms. They head for the stairs.*

The Head of the Stairs, *as the* GIRLS *reach it. A wall of fire suddenly flames up. They are compelled to turn back.*

RICARDO: This way! Follow me!

A Fourth Tier Balcony

This is just the same height as that at which the BOYS *are hanging, but there are about twelve feet between the rope and the balcony. This is a semi-long shot, showing both the balcony and the dangling* BOYS. RICARDO *and the* GIRLS—*a dozen or more of them—rush out onto the balcony.*

RICARDO *(shouts down to* ROSA*)*: Get another piece of rope!

Rosa Down Below

She darts away.

Shot of the Audience

The vaguest unrest. A little sniffing.

Backstage

ROSA *rushing in with a coil of rope. A* STAGEHAND *grabs it and throws it aloft to* HARPO.

Harpo *deftly catches the rope. Starts to tie the two ropes together.*

Fire Engines *racing through the streets.*

The Three Boys

The new rope is now attached, and they swing the end of it over to the balcony and RICARDO. *By this time the balcony itself is burning, and so are the three balconies underneath it. A* GIRL *grasps the end of the rope, and the* THREE BOYS *lower her to the ground.*

The Roof, Where the Rope Is Attached

The moorings of the rope begin to burn away.

The Balcony Again

Another GIRL *is lowered to safety. There are now only three or four left on the balcony, others having been saved meanwhile.*

On The Stage

As LOUISA *is singing,* LASSPARRI WHISPERS *to the* COUNT.
LASSPARRI: I don't like this—I'm going to get out of here.
THE COUNT *(grasping his wrist)*: You stay right where you are.
THE COUNT *picks up a musical note.*

The Rope Again

HARPO *alone on the rope, swinging a final* GIRL *to safety.*

The Roof, Where the Rope Is Attached

The moorings burn away.

Harpo Falls

A fall of about ten feet. He is bruised. They all rush to help him.

On the Stage

*The opera still proceeding—*THE COUNT SINGING. LASSPARRI *looks into the wings.*

Shot in the Wings

A curl of smoke.

Back to the Scene

LASSPARRI *(to* LOUISA, *in a heavy whisper)*: Louisa! *(She looks at him)* Let's get out of here!

He takes her hand; they make their way cautiously toward the wings, circling around in back of the ENSEMBLE MEMBERS.

The Audience, *growing more restless.*

Mrs. Claypool's Box

Disturbed, she leaves her box.

Backstage, Near Stage Door

LASSPARRI *and* LOUISA *hurrying toward the exit, as* MRS. CLAYPOOL *comes backstage.*

MRS. CLAYPOOL: Where are you going?

LASSPARRI: Do you think I'm going to stay here and get burned to death?

On Stage

THE COUNT *hits a final note; turns to where he expects* LOUISA *and* LASSPARRI *to be standing. Of course they are not there. The performance comes to a halt; the music stops.*

Backstage

    LASSPARRI, LOUISA, MRS. CLAYPOOL, GROUCHO, *and the* STAGE MANAGER.

MRS. CLAYPOOL: Signor Lassparri, you cannot do this! If we drop the curtain there will be a panic!

LASSPARRI: What do I care? Come on, Louisa!

GROUCHO *(barring the door)*: You can't do this!

Shot of the Audience

    Fire engine BELLS *are heard. That is enough for the* AUDIENCE, *which starts to leave.*

The Stage

    As the disorganized COMPANY *is also about to desert,* GROUCHO *comes out onto the stage.*

GROUCHO: Ladies and gentlemen—

The Audience *stopping in its tracks, uncertainly.*

The Stage

GROUCHO: Ladies and gentlemen, there is absolutely no danger. The fire is in the next block.

Backstage

LASSPARRI, LOUISA, MRS. CLAYPOOL, STAGE MANAGER.

STAGE MANAGER *(barring his way)*: Get back on that stage, you coward!

On Stage

GROUCHO: So if you will kindly resume your seats, the performance will go ahead immediately.

Chico Returning to His Post as Conductor

CHICO (to the MUSICIANS, who have also become disorganized): It's all right, boys. Everything okay. (He smiles at them. They feel better)

On Stage

GROUCHO (peering anxiously into the wings): While we are waiting for the performance to go ahead—

The Audience, getting out of hand again.

On Stage

GROUCHO (uneasy): I will—ah—tell you a couple of very funny stories.

Chico He LAUGHS loudly and loyally.

Backstage

LASSPARRI and LOUISA are no longer there. The STAGE MANAGER is just picking himself up from the floor.

STAGE MANAGER: What'll I do? Pull down the curtain?

MRS. CLAYPOOL (frenzied): I don't know! Mr. Driftwood!

Groucho on Stage

GROUCHO: And the Irishman says, "That was no lady, that was my wife."

Chico LAUGHING again.

The Audience, now going up the aisles in considerable disorder.

Groucho on Stage

GROUCHO (LAUGHING): Maybe you didn't get the point. Look, he can explain it to you. (Indicates CHICO)

91

The Audience Again, *in still further disorder. Then suddenly the sound of two beautiful* VOICES *is heard—clear and lovely. A few of the* AUDIENCE *stop in their tracks—then more and more.*

The Stage

GROUCHO *(takes a moment to take in the situation; then triumphantly)*: The performance is now going on!

With a wave of the hand he turns and greets RICARDO *and* ROSA, *who are just making their entrance.*

Orchestra Pit

CHICO *conducting for dear life.*

The Audience

The panic has been stopped.

Groucho Again

GROUCHO *(backing toward the wings)*: Remember—you have my personal guarantee that there is no danger. The fire is out and there is absolutely no dan—*(he is near the wings; suddenly his fanny is scorched. He backs off, with both hands covering the warm spot)* Absolutely no danger. Thank you very much.

Backstage

GROUCHO *as he comes off stage. A* FIREMAN *is playing a hose on a burning spot nearby.*

GROUCHO *(indicating the scorched spot)*: Put a little right here, please. *(The* FIREMAN *turns the hose on the desired spot)* That's fine—I'll do the same for you some time.

The Foot of the Stairs

FIREMEN *squirting water up the stairs.* HARPO *appears at the foot of the stairs; starts up.*

FIREMAN *(as* HARPO *passes him)*: You can't go up there—it's dangerous.

He tries to grab HARPO, *who tears himself loose.*

92

On Stage

The LOVERS SINGING.

Gottlieb's Office

It is now smoke-filled. HARPO *picks up the prostrate* GOTTLIEB.

Shot of the Audience, *quite enraptured by the* SINGING *of* ROSA *and* RICARDO.

Mrs. Claypool in her Box *also listening eagerly.*

The Stairs

HARPO *carrying* GOTTLIEB *down, fighting his way through fire and smoke. Halfway up, he hears a plaintive whine. He looks down.*

Close-up—a Dog

A moth-eaten MONGREL *is almost overcome by smoke.*

Back to Harpo

He drops the body of GOTTLIEB; *picks up the* DOG.

Foot of the Stairs

HARPO *comes down; quickly hands the* DOG *over to a* FIREMAN.
FIREMAN: Say, is this what you risked your life for? *(*HARPO *darts into smoke again)* Come back, you idiot! *(*HARPO *immediately reappears, staggering. He brings a chair this time; puts it down and collapses in it, winded)* Well, I hope that's all now!

HARPO *snaps his fingers in recollection; darts up again.*

On Stage

The LOVERS SINGING.

The Foot of the Stairs

HARPO *staggers down with* GOTTLIEB'S *body.*
GROUCHO: My boy, I want to congratulate you. If that was anybody but Gottlieb, you'd be a hero.

93

FIREMAN: Say, you got this fellow just in time.

On Stage, *the* SINGING *approaches a climax.*

Close-up—Chico, *smilingly conducting.*

On Stage, *the* SINGING *climaxes.*

The Audience
   Terrific APPLAUSE.

Mrs. Claypool's Box
   She is APPLAUDING *and beaming.*

Backstage GROUCHO *and* HARPO *enjoying the singers' triumph.*
GROUCHO *(to* HARPO*):* How could a fellow with a voice that big
ever get into my trunk?
   A hand descends simultaneously on the shoulder of each. The
   CAMERA PANS *to show* HENDERSON.
HENDERSON: All right, boys—now I've got you. And as soon as
this clambake is over I'm grabbing the other two.
                                              Fade out

Fade in:
   HARPO, CHICO, *and* GROUCHO, *immaculately dressed, again on
   the steps of City Hall. Around them, with smiling faces, stand*
   HENDERSON, GOTTLIEB, MRS. CLAYPOOL, RICARDO, *and* ROSA.
   POLICE *and distinguished* CITIZENS *are again in attendance;
   the* MAYOR *is speaking.*
MAYOR: —and at the risk of their own lives averted a panic and
saved three thousand people. *(*APPLAUSE*)* And so, my friends, I
take great pride in conferring honorary citizenship upon these
magnificent heroes. *(He turns to* HARPO*)* We will first hear from
Signor Tomasso.

94

HARPO, *who is standing near* GOTTLIEB, *whips out a pair of scissors with a quick gesture and snips off* GOTTLIEB'S *beard. At the same moment* CHICO *quickly smears a little glue over his chin.* HARPO *pastes on the beard and takes a glass of water.*

GROUCHO: Well, this is where I came in. Good-by everybody.

Fade out

The End

THE FILM

Interior, Hotel Dining Room in Milan
Long Shot

CAMERA PANS *a* WAITER *to* MRS. CLAYPOOL. *She's a stout dowager in a low-cut evening gown dining alone. Throughout the scene, the background is alive with* WAITERS, CIGARETTE GIRLS, *and* DINERS.

WAITER: The gentleman has not arrived yet?

MRS. CLAYPOOL: No he hasn't. What difference does it make? It's too late to dine now.

The WAITER *shrugs and leaves right, as a* BELLBOY *approaches from the rear.*

MRS. CLAYPOOL: Oh, boy!

BELLBOY: Yes, Madame?

MRS. CLAYPOOL: Will you page Mr. Otis P. Driftwood, please? *(He bows; she repeats loudly)* Mr. Otis P. Driftwood.

BELLBOY *(behind her, paging)*: Paging Mr. Driftwood. Mr. Driftwood. Mr. Driftwood. Mr. Driftwood.

As he walks off we see an attractive BLONDE *with a tinkly laugh at the table behind* MRS. CLAYPOOL. *The* MAN *facing the* BLONDE, *with his back to the* CAMERA *and to* MRS. CLAYPOOL *is* OTIS P. DRIFTWOOD (Groucho). *He turns to the* BELLBOY.

DRIFTWOOD: Boy!

Two Shot—Driftwood and Mrs. Claypool
(See film still 1.)
They are back to back, like bookends. DRIFTWOOD'S *napkin is tucked into his shirt.*

DRIFTWOOD: Will you do me a favor and stop yelling my name all over this restaurant? Do I go 'round yelling your name?

99

MRS. CLAYPOOL (*turns to* DRIFTWOOD, *whose back is still to her*): Mr. Driftwood.

Long Shot—Driftwood and Mrs. Claypool

DRIFTWOOD (*standing, and to the* BLONDE): Say, is your voice changing, or is somebody else paging me around here?

MRS. CLAYPOOL (*commandingly*): Mr. Driftwood!

With a turn of his wrist, he spins his chair to her table and sits.

DRIFTWOOD: Why, Mrs. Claypool! Helloo!

MRS. CLAYPOOL: Mr. Driftwood, you invited me to dine with you at seven o'clock. It is now eight o'clock, and no dinner.

DRIFTWOOD: What do you mean, no dinner? I just had one of the biggest meals I ever ate in my life, and no thanks to you, either.

MRS. CLAYPOOL: I've been sitting right here since seven o'clock.

DRIFTWOOD: Yes, with your back to me. When I invite a woman to dinner, I expect her to look at my face. That's the price she has to pay. (*He rolls his eyes upward*)

CAMERA PULLS BACK *to reveal* BLONDE *again, and* WAITER.

WAITER: Your check, sir.

DRIFTWOOD (WHISTLES): Nine dollars and forty cents! (*Rises*) This is an outrage! If I were you (*Drops check in front of* BLONDE), I wouldn't pay for it. (*He drops his napkin onto the table and walks between the tables and slaps* MRS. CLAYPOOL *on the back and sits to her right*) Now then, Mrs. Claypool, what are we going to have for dinner?

MRS. CLAYPOOL: You've had your dinner.

DRIFTWOOD: All right, we'll have breakfast. Waiter!

WAITER *returns, behind and between them.*

WAITER: Yes, sir.

DRIFTWOOD: Have you got any milk-fed chicken?

WAITER: Yes, sir.

DRIFTWOOD: Well, squeeze the milk out of one and bring me a glass.

WAITER: Yes, sir. (*He leaves*)

100

DRIFTWOOD *puffs on his cigar, which he has held throughout scene.*

MRS. CLAYPOOL: Mr. Driftwood, three months ago you promised to put me into society. In all that time, you've done nothing but draw a very handsome salary.

DRIFTWOOD: You think that's nothing, huh? How many men do you suppose are drawing a handsome salary nowadays? Why, you can count them on the fingers of one hand, my good woman.

MRS. CLAYPOOL: I'm not your good woman.

DRIFTWOOD: Don't say that, Mrs. Claypool. *(He takes her hand)* I don't care what your past has been. To me, you'll always be my good woman, because I love you. There, I didn't mean to tell you, but you, you dragged it out of me. I love you.

MRS. CLAYPOOL: It's rather difficult to believe that when I find you dining with another woman.

DRIFTWOOD: That woman? Do you know why I sat with her?

MRS. CLAYPOOL: No . . .

DRIFTWOOD: Because she reminded me of you.

MRS. CLAYPOOL *(she smiles toothily)*: Really?

DRIFTWOOD: Of course! That's why I'm sitting here with you, because you remind me of you. Your eyes, your throat, your lips, everything about you reminds me of you, except you. *(Her face falls)* How do you account for that? *(Turns away from her and leers toward the* CAMERA*)* If she figures that one out, she's good.

MRS. CLAYPOOL: Mr. Driftwood, I think we'd better keep everything on a business basis.

DRIFTWOOD: How do you like that? Every time I get romantic with you, you want to talk business. I don't know, there's something about me that brings out the business in every woman.

Close-up—Mrs. Claypool
She looks away, shocked at the lewdness of his remark.

Two Shot—Driftwood and Mrs. Claypool
DRIFTWOOD: All right, we'll talk business. You see that man over there eating spaghetti. . . . *(Points to right)*

Medium Close-up—Gottlieb

He is seated at a table, hidden behind a screen of spaghetti draped over a fork.

MRS. CLAYPOOL *(offscreen)*: No.

DRIFTWOOD *(offscreen)*: Well, you . . .

Two Shot—Driftwood and Mrs. Claypool

DRIFTWOOD: . . . see the spaghetti don't you? *(Turns back to her)* Now, behind that spaghetti is none other than Herman Gottlieb, Director of the New York Opera Company. Do you follow me?

MRS. CLAYPOOL: Yes.

DRIFTWOOD: Well, stop following me, or I'll have you arrested. Now, I've arranged for you to invest two hundred thousand dollars in the New York Opera Company.

MRS. CLAYPOOL: I don't understand.

DRIFTWOOD: Don't you see? You'll be a patron of the opera. You'll get into society. Then you can marry me and they'll kick you out of society. And all you've lost is two hundred thousand dollars.

Long Shot—Gottlieb Joins Them

He strides into the scene from the right, his arm extended. He is an overwhelmingly pompous man, dressed in tails and white tie, with a goatee.

GOTTLIEB *(Viennese accent)*: Ah, Mr. Driftwood!

DRIFTWOOD *rises—they shake hands.* GOTTLIEB *gives a short bow.* DRIFTWOOD *turns to introduce him to* MRS. CLAYPOOL.

DRIFTWOOD: Ah, Gottlieb. Allow me. Mrs. Claypool, Mr. Gottlieb. *(*GOTTLIEB *bows deeply)* Mr. Gottlieb, Mrs. Claypool. *(*DRIFTWOOD *bows more deeply)* Mrs. Claypool, Mr. Gottlieb. *(They trade bows)* Mr. Gottlieb, Mrs. Claypool. Mrs. Claypool, Mr. . . . *(Throughout the exchange the two men bob up and down)* I could go on like this all night, but it's tough on my suspenders. Now, where was I? Oh, yes! Mrs. Claypool, Mr. Gottlieb, *(*DRIFTWOOD

goes into an elaborate dance step as he CHANTS *the names)* Mrs.
Claypool, Mr. Gottlieb, Mrs. Claypool, Mr. Gottlieb, Mrs. Clay-
pool . . .
MRS. CLAYPOOL: What are you doing?
DRIFTWOOD: Now, if you four people want to play bridge, don't
mind me. Go right ahead.
GOTTLIEB: Mrs. Claypool, I am so happy. *(Kisses her hand)*
    As GOTTLIEB *releases her hand,* DRIFTWOOD *snatches it up,*
    rising to inspect it.
DRIFTWOOD: I just wanted to see if your rings were still there.
(He sits)
GOTTLIEB: Mrs. Claypool, you are as charming as you are beau-
tiful.
MRS. CLAYPOOL: I'm afraid you've used that speech before, Mr.
Gottlieb.

Close-up—Driftwood
DRIFTWOOD: Now listen here, Gottlieb, making love to Mrs. Claypool is my racket. What you're after is two hundred thousand
dollars.

Two Shot—Gottlieb, Standing; Mrs. Claypool, Sitting

Close-up—Driftwood
DRIFTWOOD: And you better make it plausible, because, incredible
as it may seem, Mrs. Claypool . . .

Two Shot—Gottlieb and Mrs. Claypool
DRIFTWOOD: . . . isn't as big a sap as she looks.

Close-up—Driftwood
DRIFTWOOD: How's that for love-making?

Two Shot—Mrs. Claypool and Gottlieb
MRS. CLAYPOOL: I think the Europeans do it better.

Close-up—Driftwood

DRIFTWOOD: All right, Gottlieb, it's your turn. You take a whack at it. And keep it clean.

Two Shot—Mrs. Claypool and Gottlieb

The BLONDE *is still behind them listening.*

GOTTLIEB: Oh, Mrs. Claypool, it is most generous of you to help us. Now, you have, of course, heard of Rudolfo Lassparri?

MRS. CLAYPOOL: Oh, of course.

GOTTLIEB: Oh, he's the greatest tenor since Caruso.

MRS. CLAYPOOL: Yes.

GOTTLIEB: Tonight, with the money you so generously provide, I sign . . .

Close-up—Driftwood

He raises his eyebrows and sticks his tongue out.

GOTTLIEB *(offscreen)*: . . . Lassparri for the Opera Company. He will be a . . .

Two Shot—Mrs. Claypool and Gottlieb

GOTTLIEB: . . . sensation. All New York will be at your feet. *(He extends his arms)*

Long Shot—All Three of Them

DRIFTWOOD: Well, there's plenty of room. *(He lifts up tablecloth and looks under table at her feet)*

GOTTLIEB: And now, the opera awaits us. If you both will honor me by occupying my box.

MRS. CLAYPOOL *rises.* GOTTLIEB *drapes her coat around her shoulders.*

MRS. CLAYPOOL: I should be charmed.

GOTTLIEB: And you, Mr. Driftwood?

DRIFTWOOD: Well, I'll join up with you later. *(*GOTTLIEB *takes her arm)* And listen, Gottlieb, nix on the love-making, because I saw Mrs. Claypool first. Of course, her mother really saw her first, but there's no point in bringing the Civil War into this.

Fade out

Fade in:

Interior, Opera House

Wide Shot—the Audience
CAMERA *is* SHOOTING *toward the stage and includes the* AUDI-ENCE *and three tiers of boxes.*

Interior, Dressing Room
TOMASSO (Harpo) *is reflected in a make-up mirror. He's dressed as Pagliacci. He beats his chest—throws out his arms—tries to sing—nothing. He shakes his head—shrugs—sprays his throat and tries again—nothing. He shrugs and sprays more vigorously. He turns away from the reflection and tries to look busy.*

Medium Long Shot—Lassparri and Tomasso
The door opens and LASSPARRI, *carrying a walking stick and dressed in street clothes, enters. He strides over to* TOMASSO.
LASSPARRI: What are you doing in my costume? *(Strikes* TOMASSO *with his stick)* Take it off at once, do you hear? Immediately. *(*HARPO *sheds the clown suit, beneath which is* LIEUTENANT PINKERTON's *naval uniform. He salutes* LASSPARRI*)* Why, you . . . *(Moves toward* TOMASSO *threateningly)* . . . you . . . *(Throws* TOMASSO *against the wall)*

Medium Shot—Tomasso
He is hurled against the wall.

Medium Shot—Lassparri
He scowls at TOMASSO.
LASSPARRI: Take that off.

105

Medium Shot—Tomasso

He kicks off his trousers, and peels off his coat, revealing a peasant girl's dress. He shakes down the skirt and a beatific, feminine look comes over his face.

Medium Shot—Lassparri

Angrier than ever, he begins to chase TOMASSO *around a chair.*
LASSPARRI: Take off that dress! Do you hear me? You dumb idiot, you do as I say or I'll break your neck. (TOMASSO, *grinning flirtatiously, moves from left to right keeping the chair between them*) Do you hear me? (TOMASSO *goes behind a trunk knocking over some suitcases*) Take off that dress! (TOMASSO *holds up both hands with fingers crossed, as if it were a children's game, and further infuriates* LASSPARRI) If I get my hands on you, you'll never hear the end of this. (TOMASSO *drops the dress;* LASSPARRI *picks up a whip*)

Close-up—Tomasso

He hides behind a curtain and wraps it around himself demurely.
LASSPARRI: You're no longer my dresser. You're fired! *(See film still 2.)* Get out! (LASSPARRI *beats* TOMASSO *with the whip, driving him out of the room*) Get out! Get out, do you hear me? Out you go! And don't come back in here again.

Exterior, Hallway

Medium Shot—Tomasso

TOMASSO *falls into hallway as* LASSPARRI *slams the door shut.*
   CAMERA PANS UP LEFT *to reveal* ROSA *standing outside her dressing-room door. She looks sympathetically at* TOMASSO *sprawled on the floor. She crosses to him, kneels and puts an arm around him.*
ROSA: Don't you care. You're lucky to be rid of him.
They rise as LASSPARRI *rushes into the hall.*
LASSPARRI *(oily)*: Oh . . . good evening, Rosa.

106

ROSA: Good evening, signore.

LASSPARRI: Tomasso, why don't you come in? I've been waiting for you.

TOMASSO *glances at* ROSA *and is led into dressing room by* LASSPARRI. ROSA, *disturbed, leaves. The hallway is empty, but from inside* LASSPARRI'*s dressing room we hear what* SOUNDS *like* LASSPARRI *beating* TOMASSO.

Interior, Rosa's Dressing Room

ROSA *enters; crosses to* MAID *who hands her a corsage.*

MAID: Are they not beautiful, signorine? From Signor Lassparri.

ROSA: I wouldn't wear them if they were the only flowers in the world. *(*KNOCK *at door)* Come in. *(Angrily she throws the corsage into wastebasket)*

Door opens. RICARDO, *a handsome young chorus member, stands in the doorway.*

RICARDO: Oh, no, not if you're going to use that tone. Now, let's try the whole thing over again, only this time try to be a little more cordial. *(Closes door—*KNOCKS *again)*

ROSA *(smiles delightedly)*: Come in.

RICARDO *(he opens door)*: Ah, that's better. Now, let's try it once more.

ROSA: No, Ricky! You're such a fool.

She crosses to him, takes his arm and pulls him into the room. The MAID *busies herself behind a screen while they speak.*

RICARDO: Now, what was it you wanted to see me about?

ROSA: Oh, I suppose I sent for you.

RICARDO: Well, you meant to. Didn't she, Marie?

MAID *(she reappears from behind the screen)*: Uh-huh. *(She leaves the room)*

ROSA *sits at dressing table.* RICARDO *stands behind her with his hands on her shoulders.*

RICARDO: Now look—here it is the last night of the season and I'm more in love with you than ever. Now, what are you going to do about it?

Rosa: Now, Ricardo, we have all summer to talk that over. To-night we have to sing an opera.
Ricardo: Have to sing an opera! *You* have to sing an opera. I'm nothing but a glorified chorus man.
He turns away from her and walks to right.
Rosa: Don't say that.
She rises and steps toward him. They face each other.
Ricardo: I've got to say it, and I've got something else to say. What are you doing tonight? Unless that big ham Lassparri has asked you first.
Rosa: He has asked me first.
Ricardo: Just my luck.
Rosa: But I'm having supper with you, Ricardo.
Ricardo: Hurray! We'll have champagne, music, flowers. *(He pulls the flowers from wastebasket and reads the card)* Lassparri. Oh, no. No flowers.
He tosses flowers behind the dressing screen. Rosa LAUGHS, *and they join hands.*

Interior, Backstage
Fiorello (Chico) KNOCKS *on an open door. The* Doorman, *who is sorting mail, turns to him. In the background we can hear the chorus performing* Pagliacci.
Doorman: Well, Fiorello. *(*Fiorello LAUGHS, *they shake hands)*
Fiorello: Tony!
Doorman: Where have you been all these weeks?
Fiorello: Oh, here, there—different places. You gotta some mail for me?
Doorman: Mail for you? You don't work here.
Fiorello: All right, where am I gonna getta my mail? I no work any place. *(They* LAUGH*)*

Medium Long Shot—Tomasso
He is at the top of a metal spiral staircase. He's wearing a top hat. He WHISTLES *to* Fiorello.

Medium Close-up—Fiorello

With his back to CAMERA, *he looks up at* TOMASSO.

FIORELLO: Hey . . . *(Throws his arms in the air)*

Medium Long Shot—Tomasso at the Top of the Stairs

He points at FIORELLO, *throws his arms wide and makes a "shh" gesture with a finger to his lips, puts his hands on the bannister and begins a frantic and speeded-up descent. He hits the floor on his knees and makes yet another circle around the base of the stairs. He rises and spins into* FIORELLO's *arms. They embrace and make mysterious private gestures to one another, and then embrace again.*

FIORELLO: Tomasso! Hey, not so good. Don't be so glad. I brought you present. *(*TOMASSO *shakes his head excitedly)* You got something for me too? What you got? *(*FIORELLO *produces a salami from his jacket—*TOMASSO *does likewise—they trade gifts)* Where's Ricardo? *(*TOMASSO *points toward stage)* All right. Shh! *(*TOMASSO *makes "shh" gesture again)*

FIORELLO *exits left toward stage area.* TOMASSO *turns, back to* CAMERA, *and starts to mount the circular staircase. He changes his mind when he sees a fire ax on the wall. He puts the salami on top of a barrel, takes the ax and noisily chops the salami in half. (See film still 3.) He "shh's" himself as the* CHORUS *continues in the background. He takes one bite from each half of the salami and then goes up the stairs.*

The Stage—Lassparri, Rosa, and the Chorus

He is in his Pagliacci costume, BANGING *on a drum and* SINGING *his way into the hearts of the audience.*

LASSPARRI, ROSA and CHORUS:

> Evviva, evviva, evviva!
> (Hurray, hurray, hurray!)
> Evviva il principe . . .
> (Hurray for the prince . . .)

109

Interior, Backstage (the Wings):
Full Shot Favoring Fiorello

The Chorus Members *come backstage.* Ricardo *enters and goes right to* Fiorello. *They greet each other warmly and shake hands.*

RICARDO: Fiorello!

FIORELLO: Ricardo!

RICARDO: What are you doing here? I thought you were out with the circus.

FIORELLO: The circus? When was I with the circus? Oh, I nearly forgot. That was a long time ago—last week. Why, since then I have lots of jobs.

RICARDO: Yeah, your piano and my voice. You know, all those years we studied at the conservatory, and what's come of it?

FIORELLO: Aw, what's the matter with you? We're still young. We got our health. *(*FIORELLO *looks over to stage)*

Two Shot—Lassparri and Rosa

LASSPARRI *(*SINGS*)*: Grande spettacolo a venti tre ore.

                (Great spectacle at eleven o'clock.)

He's still on stage BEATING *his drum and* SINGING. ROSA *is next to him.*

Two Shot—Ricardo and Fiorello

FIORELLO: You hear that? Some day, Ricardo, you're going to be where Lassparri is. Why, when you were a little boy six years old, you sing better than Lassparri.

RICARDO: Yeah. Maybe I was better at six than I am now.

FIORELLO: Aw, you make me sick. You crazy. Why, you sing better than Lassparri ever could sing and you know it.

RICARDO: All right, I know it and you know it, but the public doesn't know it.

FIORELLO: All right, we tell the public.

RICARDO: How?

110

FIORELLO: What you need is a manager . . . a wise guy . . . somebody who'sa very smart. Hey, I know just the man for you.

RICARDO: You do? Who is it?

FIORELLO: Me. *(They* LAUGH*)*

RICARDO: But you wouldn't make any money at it.

FIORELLO: All right, I break even. Just as long as I no lose nothing.

RICARDO: Don't worry. Fine.

Exterior, Opera House

DRIFTWOOD, *puffing on his cigar, pulls up in a horse-drawn carriage. A* DOORMAN *walks briskly to the carriage.*

DRIFTWOOD *(to* DOORMAN*)*: Is the opera over yet?

DOORMAN: Not yet, signor. In a few minutes.

DRIFTWOOD *(to* DRIVER*)*: Hey, you! I told you to slow that nag down. On account of you I nearly heard the opera. Now then, once around the park and drive slowly. And none of your back talk.

The carriage pulls away; the DOORMAN *watches it go.*

Interior, Opera House

ROSA *is onstage* SINGING.

ROSA *(*SINGS*)*:

> Vanno laggiu
> (They go over there)
> Verso un paese strano . . .
> (To a strange country . . .)

Two Shot—Ricardo and Fiorello

Backstage, they are watching ROSA *from the wings. Her* VOICE *continues over their dialogue.*

FIORELLO: You're still crazy about her? And she's crazy about you, too?

RICARDO: Even if she was, I couldn't ask her to marry me.

111

FIORELLO: Hey, don't worry. The manager—he's a fix everything. Anyhow, we're together again, you and me, justa like old times, eh?

RICARDO: Yeah, like old times.

FIORELLO: Ah, you betta my life.

Long Shot—Rosa

She is onstage, SINGING.

ROSA (SINGS): E van. E van. E van. E . . .
    (They go. They go. They go. They . . .)

Another Angle—Rosa

ROSA (SINGS): . . . van!
    (. . . go!)
At the final notes of her aria the AUDIENCE *begins to* APPLAUD.

Long Shot—Audience Applauding

Two Shot—Gottlieb and Mrs. Claypool

They're in MRS. CLAYPOOL's *box. They rise and he helps her on with her coat.*

GOTTLIEB: If you'll pardon my saying so, Mrs. Claypool, Mr. Driftwood seems to me hardly the person to handle your business affairs.

MRS. CLAYPOOL: I'm beginning to think the same thing.

    DRIFTWOOD, *in full formal dress, enters the box,* APPLAUDING *wildly.*

DRIFTWOOD: Bravo! Bravo! Bravo! Bravo! Bravo! Bravo! Well, I made it. How soon does the curtain go up?

    He removes his hat and sits between GOTTLIEB *and* MRS. CLAYPOOL *who are standing.*

GOTTLIEB: The curtain, Mr. Driftwood, will go up again next season.

MRS. CLAYPOOL: You've missed the entire opera.

DRIFTWOOD: Well, I only missed it by a few minutes. Then I can go then, eh? *(He turns to talk to attractive* WOMAN *in the next box)*

GOTTLIEB: Well, Mrs. Claypool, was I right? Isn't Lassparri the greatest tenor that ever lived?

MRS. CLAYPOOL: He's superb, but what would you have to pay him?

> *The* WOMAN *leaves.* DRIFTWOOD *leans on the balcony railing and looks down at the* AUDIENCE. GOTTLIEB *and* MRS. CLAY-POOL *continue* TALKING.

GOTTLIEB: What's the difference? He must sail with us tomorrow, no matter how much we pay him. Why, he would be worth a thousand dollars a night.

DRIFTWOOD *(throws his hat over railing and stands up suddenly)*: How much?

GOTTLIEB: A thousand dollars a night.

DRIFTWOOD: A thousand dollars a night! What does he do? *(He sits on railing)*

GOTTLIEB: What does he do? He sings!

DRIFTWOOD: And you're willing to pay him a thousand dollars a night just for singing? Why, you can get a phonograph record of "Minnie the Moocher" for seventy-five cents.

MRS. CLAYPOOL: Oh!

DRIFTWOOD: For a buck and a quarter, you can get Minnie.

GOTTLIEB: Well, if you'll excuse me, Mrs. Claypool, I think I had better arrange to see Lassparri immediately. You are agreed—a thousand dollars a night?

MRS. CLAYPOOL: Just as you think.

DRIFTWOOD *(to himself)*: A thousand dollars a night! There must be some way I can get a piece of this. *(He turns back to* GOTTLIEB *and* MRS. CLAYPOOL*)* Wait a minute. Why don't I sign Lassparri? I represent Mrs. Claypool.

GOTTLIEB: But I represent the New York Opera Company. Now, boy *(*MESSENGER *enters)*, will you give my card to Signor Lassparri, please? *(He hands him a card. The* MESSENGER *leaves)*

Dissolve to:
Interior, Backstage

Medium Shot—Tomasso

SHOOTING *over his shoulder toward several* CHORUS MEMBERS *waiting in the wings. He hurries toward them carrying a covered silver dish. He pushes his way through the* CROWD *searching for someone.*

Medium Shot—Favoring Tomasso

He makes his way to LASSPARRI, *still in costume and surrounded by* ADMIRERS. TOMASSO WHISTLES *to get* LASSPARRI'S *attention.*

Medium Close Shot—Lassparri

He reacts angrily to TOMASSO'S WHISTLE.
LASSPARRI: What is it? What do you want?
TOMASSO *presents the covered tray and then opens it.* LASSPARRI *takes* GOTTLIEB'S *card while* TOMASSO *ogles a* BLONDE *who gives him a dirty look.* TOMASSO *shrugs and leaves as* LASSPARRI *reads the card.*

Close-up—Insert

The card reads:

> May I see you?
> HERMAN GOTTLIEB
> MANAGING DIRECTOR
> NEW YORK OPERA COMPANY

Medium Shot—Lassparri

He looks at the card and crosses to ROSA *who is talking with* RICARDO *and the other* CAST MEMBERS. *As* LASSPARRI *speaks to her he pulls her a few feet away.* RICARDO *remains in view, listening.*
LASSPARRI: Rosa.

114

ROSA: Yes, signore?

LASSPARRI: My good friend, Herman Gottlieb is coming back to see me. How would you like to have supper with us?

ROSA: I'm terribly sorry, Signor Lassparri. I already have an engagement.

LASSPARRI: Oh, I see. Well, that's too bad, because I have an idea he's going to invite me to sing in New York, and, ahh, he may permit me to select my leading lady. Are you sure you can't break your appointment?

ROSA: I'm terribly sorry, signore.

> *She turns away from* LASSPARRI *and takes* RICARDO'S *arm. They exit right.* LASSPARRI *looks chagrined and walks over to* TOMASSO, *who is pounding the silver cover on the tray and* BLOWING *a whistle. He grabs* TOMASSO *and jerks him to his feet.* DRIFTWOOD *enters behind them and to their left.*

LASSPARRI: What do you mean by humiliating me in front of all those people? *(He slaps* TOMASSO*)* You're fired. Do you understand? You're fired! *(He slaps him again as* DRIFTWOOD *watches)*

DRIFTWOOD: Hey, you big bully, what's the idea of hitting that little bully?

LASSPARRI: Will you kindly let me handle my own affairs? *(He slaps* TOMASSO *again)* Get out! *(He pushes him away)*

Two Shot—Driftwood and Lassparri

LASSPARRI: Now what have you got to say to me?

DRIFTWOOD: Just this—can you sleep on your stomach with such big buttons on your pajamas? *(He pulls a pom-pom off* LASSPARRI'S *costume)*

LASSPARRI: Why you . . .

> *As* LASSPARRI *winds up to hit* DRIFTWOOD, TOMASSO *hits him on the head from behind with a hammer, knocking him out. They lay out the body.*

Three Shot—Driftwood, Lassparri, and Tomasso

TOMASSO *pulls a bottle from his pocket, holding it under* LASS-

115

PARRI's *nose.* DRIFTWOOD's *head is cut off at top of* FRAME *as he watches this.*

DRIFTWOOD: Nice work. I think you got him. Ah, smelling salts. That'll bring him to. You're sorry for what you did, eh? That shows a nice spirit. Now he's coming along. Yeah, he'll be fine now.

LASSPARRI *nods slightly.*

TOMASSO *hits* LASSPARRI *with mallet again and as his head falls back,* DRIFTWOOD *slips the mallet under his head as a pillow.* TOMASSO *runs off scared.* DRIFTWOOD *places his left foot on* LASSPARRI's *body.*

DRIFTWOOD: Get fresh with me, eh?

DRIFTWOOD *flicks ashes on* LASSPARRI *as* FIORELLO *walks in from left.*

FIORELLO: How do you do?

DRIFTWOOD: Hello.

FIORELLO: What's the matter, Mister?

DRIFTWOOD: Oh, we had an argument and he pulled a knife on me, so I shot him.

FIORELLO: Do you mind if I . . . (FIORELLO *puts his left foot on* LASSPARRI. DRIFTWOOD *and* FIORELLO *stand there, one foot each on* LASSPARRI, *as if they were at a bar*)

(See film still 4.)

DRIFTWOOD: No, no, go right ahead. Plenty of room.

Two Shot—Fiorello and Driftwood

DRIFTWOOD: Two beers, bartender.

FIORELLO: I'll take two beers, too.

DRIFTWOOD: Well, things seem to be getting better around the country.

FIORELLO: I don't know. I'm a stranger here myself.

DRIFTWOOD: Say, I just remembered. I came back here looking for somebody. You don't know who it is, do you?

FIORELLO: It's a funny thing. It just slipped my mind.

DRIFTWOOD: Oh, I know—I know. The greatest tenor in the world —that's what I'm after.

116

FIORELLO: Well, I'm his manager.

DRIFTWOOD: Whose manager?

FIORELLO: The greatest tenor in the world.

DRIFTWOOD: The fellow that sings at the opera here?

FIORELLO: Sure.

DRIFTWOOD: What's his name?

FIORELLO: What do you care? I can't pronounce it. What do you want with him?

DRIFTWOOD: Well, uh, I want to sign him up for the New York Opera Company. Do you know that America is waiting to hear him sing?

FIORELLO: Well, he can sing loud, but he can't sing that loud.

Close-up—Driftwood

DRIFTWOOD: Well, I think I can get America to meet him half-way. Could he sail tomorrow?

Two Shot—Fiorello and Driftwood

FIORELLO: You pay him enough money he could sail yesterday. How much you pay him?

DRIFTWOOD (to himself): Well, I don't know. Let's see . . . a thousand dollars a night. I'm entitled to a small profit. How about ten dollars a night?

FIORELLO (he LAUGHS scornfully): Ten—ten dollars! I'll take it.

Close-up—Driftwood

DRIFTWOOD (puffing on a cigar): All right, but remember, I get ten per cent for negotiating the deal.

Two Shot—Fiorello and Driftwood

FIORELLO: Yes, and I get ten per cent for being the manager. How much does that leave?

DRIFTWOOD: Well, that leaves him, uh, eight dollars.

FIORELLO: Eight dollars, eh? Well, he sends a five dollars home to his mother.

117

DRIFTWOOD: Well, that leaves three dollars.

FIORELLO: Three dollars. Can he live in New York on three dollars?

DRIFTWOOD: Like a prince. Of course, he won't be able to eat, but he can live like a prince. However, out of that three dollars, you know, he'll have to pay an income tax.

FIORELLO: Oh, his income tax, eh?

DRIFTWOOD: Yes. You know, there's a Federal tax and a state tax and a city tax and a street tax and a sewer tax.

FIORELLO: How much does this come to?

DRIFTWOOD: Well, I figure if he doesn't sing too often he can break even.

FIORELLO: All right, we take it.

DRIFTWOOD: All right, fine. Now, uh, here are the contracts. (*He pulls contracts from his inside jacket pocket*) You just put his name at the top and, uh, and you sign at the bottom. There's no need of you reading that because these are duplicates. (DRIFTWOOD *unfurls his copy as if it were a banner. They stand there, each looking at a copy of a very official contract*)

(*See film still 5.*)

FIORELLO: Yes, duplicates. Duplicates, eh?

DRIFTWOOD: I say, they're—they're duplicates.

FIORELLO: Oh, sure, it's a duplicate. Certainly.

DRIFTWOOD: Don't you know what duplicates are?

FIORELLO: Sure. Those five kids up in Canada.

Close-up—Driftwood

DRIFTWOOD: Well, I wouldn't know about that. I haven't been in Canada in years.

Two Shot—Fiorello and Driftwood

DRIFTWOOD: Well, go ahead and read it.

FIORELLO: What does it say?

DRIFTWOOD: Well, go on and read it.

FIORELLO: All right—you read it.
DRIFTWOOD: All right. I'll read it to you.

Close-up—Driftwood
DRIFTWOOD: Can you hear?

Close-up—Fiorello
FIORELLO: I haven't heard anything yet. Did you say anything?

Close-up—Driftwood
DRIFTWOOD: Well, I haven't said anything worth hearing.

Close-up—Fiorello
FIORELLO: Well, that's why I didn't hear anything.

Close-up—Driftwood
DRIFTWOOD: Well, that's why I didn't say anything.

Two Shot—Fiorello and Driftwood
DRIFTWOOD *studies contract.* FIORELLO *stares at him suspiciously as* DRIFTWOOD *holds the contract close to his face, then moves it away.*
FIORELLO: Can you read?
DRIFTWOOD: I can read but I can't see it. I don't seem . . . *(He holds it farther away)* . . . to have it in focus here. If my arms were a little longer, I could read it. You haven't got a baboon in your pocket have you? Here—here—here we are. Now, I've got it. Now, pay particular attention to this first clause because it's most important. Says the—uh—the party of the first part shall be known in this contract as the party of the first part. How do you like that? That's pretty neat, eh?
FIORELLO: No, that's no good.
DRIFTWOOD: What's the matter with it?

119

FIORELLO: I don't know. Let's hear it again.

DRIFTWOOD: Says the—uh—the party of the first part should be known in this contract as the party of the first part.

FIORELLO: That sounds a little better this time.

DRIFTWOOD: Well, it grows on you. Would you like to hear it once more?

FIORELLO: Uh, just the first part.

DRIFTWOOD: What do you mean? The—the party of the first part?

FIORELLO: No, the first part of the party of the first part.

DRIFTWOOD: All right. It says the—uh—the first part of the party of the first part, should be known in this contract as the first part of the party of the first part, should be known in this contract— look. Why should we quarrel about a thing like this? We'll take it right out, eh? *(DRIFTWOOD rips off the top of contract)*

FIORELLO: Yeah. *(He rips off the top of his copy)* It's too long anyhow. Now, what have we got left?

DRIFTWOOD: Well, I've got about a foot and a half. Now, it says, uh, the party of the second part shall be known in this contract as the party of the second part.

FIORELLO: Well, I don't know about that.

DRIFTWOOD: Now, what's the matter?

FIORELLO: I no like the second party either.

DRIFTWOOD: Well, you should have come to the first party. We didn't get home till around four in the morning. I was blind for three days.

FIORELLO: Hey, look! Why can't the first part of the second party be the second part of the first party? Then you got something.

DRIFTWOOD: Well, look, uh, rather than go through all that again, what do you say?

FIORELLO: Fine. *(They rip together)*

DRIFTWOOD: Now, uh, now, I've got something here you're bound to like. You'll be crazy about it.

FIORELLO: No, I don't like it.

DRIFTWOOD: You don't like what?

120

1

2

3

4

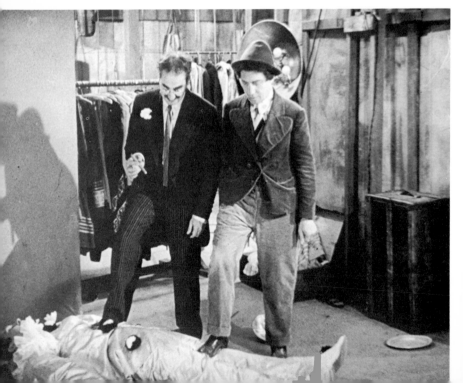

5

6 7

8

9

10

11

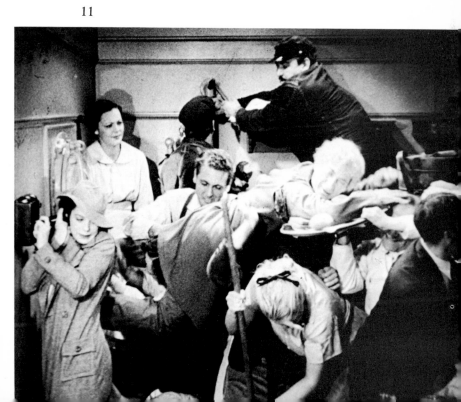

12

13

14

15

16

17

18

19

20

21

22

23

24

25

26

27

28

29

30

31

32

33

FIORELLO: Whatever it is . . . I don't like it.

DRIFTWOOD: Well, don't lets break up an old friendship over a thing like that. Ready?

FIORELLO: Okay. *(They rip together)* Now the next part, I don't think you're going to like.

DRIFTWOOD: Well, your word's good enough for me. *(They both rip)* Now, then, is my word good enough for you?

FIORELLO: I should say not.

DRIFTWOOD: Well, that takes out two more clauses. *(They both tear two strips)* Now the party of the eighth part . . .

FIORELLO: No.

DRIFTWOOD: No?

FIORELLO: No. That's no good. *(They both rip again)* No.

 DRIFTWOOD *gives him a dirty look.*

DRIFTWOOD: The party of the ninth . . .

FIORELLO: No, that's no good too. *(They rip again)* Hey, how is it my contract is skinnier than yours?

DRIFTWOOD: Well, I don't know. You must have been out on a tear last night. But, anyhow, we're all set now, aren't we?

FIORELLO: Oh, sure.

DRIFTWOOD: Now, just, uh, just you put your name right down there and then the deal is—is—uh, legal.

FIORELLO: I forgot to tell you. I can't write.

DRIFTWOOD: Well, that's all right. There's no ink in the pen anyhow. But, listen, it's a contract, isn't it?

FIORELLO: Oh, sure.

DRIFTWOOD: We've got a contract?

FIORELLO: You bet. . . .

DRIFTWOOD: No matter how small it is.

FIORELLO: Hey, wait—wait! What does this say here? This thing here?

DRIFTWOOD: Oh, that? Oh, that's the usual clause. That's in every contract. That just says, uh, it says, uh *(He reads from FIORELLO's contract)* if any of the parties participating in this contract is shown

121

not to be in their right mind, the entire agreement is automatically nullified.

FIORELLO: Well, I don't know.

DRIFTWOOD: It's all right. That's—that's in every contract. That's —that's what they call a sanity clause.

FIORELLO: You can't fool me. There ain't no Sanity Claus.

DRIFTWOOD: Well, you win the white carnation. Sanity Claus.

Long Shot—Fiorello, Driftwood, and Lassparri
LASSPARRI *is still on the floor, out cold.*

FIORELLO: I give this to RICARDO.

He walks away and encounters GOTTLIEB *with* MRS. CLAYPOOL.

GOTTLIEB: . . . Sensation in New York. Uh, pardon me, could you tell me where Signor Lassparri is?

FIORELLO: Sure. There's Lassparri. *(He points to* LASSPARRI *flat on his back)*

GOTTLIEB: Lassparri! *(He runs to the prostrate* LASSPARRI*)*

Two Shot—Fiorello and Driftwood
DRIFTWOOD: Lassparri! Then who did I sign?

FIORELLO: You signed Ricardo Baroni, that's my man.

Two Shot—Gottlieb and Lassparri
GOTTLIEB *helps* LASSPARRI *into a sitting position.*

GOTTLIEB: Signor Lassparri. What's happened?

Close-up—Tomasso
He's hiding behind a stage flat. He uncurls a rope.

GOTTLIEB *(offscreen)*: Speak to me. It's me. It's Gottlieb! Speak to me!

Close-up—a Flying Sandbag

Two Shot—Gottlieb and Lassparri
GOTTLIEB: It's me! It's Gottlieb . . .

The sandbag falls on LASSPARRI'S *head, knocking him out again.*
GOTTLIEB: Oh. What is this now? *(He looks up to see where the sandbag came from)*

Two Shot—Fiorello and Driftwood
TOMASSO, *smiling, joins them.*
DRIFTWOOD: How early the fruit is falling this season.

Fade out

Fade in:
Music up.

Exterior, Docks

A Sign

> SAILING TODAY
> *S. S. Americus*
> FIRST-CLASS PASSENGERS
> *This Way*

MIDSHIPMEN *and* LONGSHOREMEN *pass in and out of the frame.*

Dissolve to:
Medium Long Shot—the Dock
*Gangplank—*PASSENGERS *boarding.*

Dissolve to:
High Angle—Shooting Toward Bottom of the Gangplank
CAMERA PANS *to follow* MRS. CLAYPOOL *and* DRIFTWOOD *as they board the ship.* DRIFTWOOD *drags a trunk.*
MRS. CLAYPOOL: Are you sure you have everything, Otis?
DRIFTWOOD: I've never had any complaints yet.

123

Two Shot—Ricardo and Rosa

They're in the CROWD *on the dock. They walk toward the gangplank, arm in arm.*

RICARDO: Well, here you are—on your way to America and fame.

Close-up—Rosa

SHOOTING OVER RICARDO's *shoulder.*

ROSA: Oh, Ricardo, I'm going to miss you.

RICARDO: How do you think I feel about it?

GOTTLIEB *(offscreen)*: Ah, Miss Castaldi! All ready for *(He enters right)* the big trip?

ROSA: Oh, Mr. Gottlieb. This is Ricardo Baroni of the Opera Company.

RICARDO: How do you do.

GOTTLIEB: Baroni? Did you say Baroni? *(He LAUGHS)*

RICARDO: Is it as funny as all that?

GOTTLIEB: Mr. Otis P. Driftwood seems to think that you have quite a voice.

RICARDO: Yes—really I have.

GOTTLIEB: Well, that's interesting. *(*LASSPARRI, *in black suit and gray fedora, strides forward from left)* Ah, Lassparri's come.

A crowd of admirers follows LASSPARRI. *They engulf* ROSA *and* GOTTLIEB, *separating them from* RICARDO.

LASSPARRI: Rosa!

MUSICIAN: Come on, Ricardo. Come on.

RICARDO: No, thanks.

Medium Shot—Top of the Gangplank—Rosa and Lassparri

They are boarding.

ROSA *(flowers in her hand)*: Come on, Ricky!

Medium Shot—Ricardo

He looks up at the ship forlornly.

Medium Shot—Rosa

She looks down over the railing at RICARDO.

Medium Shot—Lassparri and Gottlieb

They're at the railing, waving to the CROWD.

Medium Long Shot—the Crowd

LASSPARRI's *point of view, looking down at the* CROWD.
CROWD: Sing Lassparri! Sing Lassparri!

Medium Shot—Lassparri

He bows. A WOMAN *approaches from behind.*
WOMAN: Monsieur Lassparri.
LASSPARRI: Yes?
WOMAN: Will you give us a farewell song?
CROWD *(offscreen)*: Oh, please!

Medium Close Shot—Lassparri

LASSPARRI: My dear friends, I am so sorry. I must be excused
but—I have a slight touch of laryngitis. *(The* CROWD *groans in
disappointment as he turns to* GOTTLIEB*)* Why should I sing for
them when I'm not being paid for it?
  A VOICE *says* "Where's Rosa?" *The* CROWD *moves away to
  right.*

Medium Shot—Rosa

The CROWD *enters asking her to sing—ad libs.*

Long Shot—the Dock

RICARDO *is in the background looking up at the ship.*

Medium Shot—Rosa

The CROWD *surrounds her.*
ROSA: Yes, of course I'll sing.

125

Close-up—Rosa

She begins to SING.

ROSA *(SINGING)*:

> I'll see you each dream I dream
> With every loving sigh
> I'll count the hours that we're apart
> For here am I . . .

Medium Shot—Ricardo

*He smiles up at her, lurking among the trunks.
(See film still 6.)*

Close-up—Rosa

ROSA *(SINGING)*:

> . . . Alone
> Alone, with a sky of romance above . . .

Medium Shot—Ricardo

Still smiling, he walks forward as he realizes that she is SING-
ING *to him.*

ROSA *(SINGING)*:

> . . . Alone
> Alone when you whisper good-by, my love . . .

Medium Close-up—Rosa

ROSA *(SINGING)*:

> . . . But I will still remember
> The happiness we've known . . .

Medium Shot—Ricardo

He climbs onto a pile of trunks.

Medium Shot—Rosa

ROSA *(SINGING)*:

> . . . And though I may be alone
> I'm not . . .

Rosa *(singing)*:

> . . . Alone—as long as I find you in every dream
> I know I'll see you each night in
> The starlight's gleam
> And in those magic moments
> I'll have you for my own
> Alone, till we are together
> We two . . . Alone . . .

Medium Long Shot—the Dock

As she sings *a dolly loaded with luggage pulls in front of* Ricardo.

Close-up—Ricardo

Ricardo *(singing)*:

> Alone—alone with a sky of romance above
> Alone, alone when you whisper
> Good-by, my love.
> But I will still remember
> The happiness we've known . . .

Medium Close-up—Rosa

She looks down toward Ricardo.

Ricardo *(offscreen,* singing*)*:

> . . . And though I may be alone . . .

Close-up—Ricardo

Ricardo *(singing)*:

> . . . I'm not alone as long
> As I find you in every dream . . .

Close-up—Rosa

She looks around and walks off. We hear Ricardo *continuing to* sing, *more faintly now.*

Medium Shot—Gottlieb

He listens thoughtfully to RICARDO's SINGING.

ROSA *(entering)*: Oh, Mr. Gottlieb, hasn't he a wonderful voice? There must be a place for him in New York.

GOTTLIEB: Not a bad voice. Some day, perhaps, when he has made a reputation.

Medium Long Shot—the Dock

The dolly moves off revealing RICARDO *alone.*

RICARDO *(*SINGING*)*:

> . . . Alone till we are together
> We two . . .

Close-up—Ricardo

RICARDO *(*SINGING*)*:

> A — h-h-h — l — o-o-o — n — e-e-e!

Medium Close-up—Rosa

She looks down over the railing at him and smiles.

Interior, the Poop Deck

The CROWD *mills about—*FIORELLO *and* TOMASSO *run down the ladder,* FIORELLO YELLING *"Rosa."* TOMASSO HONKS *his horn and they run off.*

STEWARD: All visitors on shore! All visitors on shore!

FIORELLA: Rosa!

Medium Long Shot—the Deck

ROSA *turns as* FIORELLO *rushes in right and embraces her. We can still hear* RICARDO SINGING *from the dock.* TOMASSO *runs in right and jumps on both of them. Then* TOMASSO *moves down the railing kissing all the passengers, finally including a* SHIP'S OFFICER *in a large embrace.* FIORELLO *pushes* TOMASSO *off.*

ROSA: Fiorello.

FIORELLO: Ah, we've come to say good-by to you. Hey, come on.

Close-up—Ricardo

He's still on the dock, he's still singing, and he's still looking up.

RICARDO *(SINGING)*:

> . . . But I will still remember
> The happiness I've known . . .

Medium Shot—Rosa

She runs to the railing and makes it a DUET.

ROSA *(SINGING)*:

> . . . And though I may be alone
> I'm not.

Long Shot—the Dock

View from the ship of the assembled multitude on the dock. The CROWD *joins in the song.*

Medium Long Shot—the Gangplank

MUSICIANS PLAY *as they stroll down the gangplank.*

Medium Shot—the Ship

A SHIP'S OFFICER *orders the gangplank taken away.*

OFFICER: All right. Take it away.

SAILOR: Yes, sir.

Medium Shot—the Deck

The CROWD *is pushed aside by* DRIFTWOOD *as he makes his way to the top of the gangplank just before it's pushed away.*

DRIFTWOOD: Hey, have I got time to go back and pay my hotel bill?

OFFICER: Sorry . . . too late.

DRIFTWOOD: That suits me fine.

129

DRIFTWOOD *slouches away from the* OFFICER, *back into the* CROWD.

Medium Close-up—Rosa
She is still at the railing, still smiling. We HEAR *the chorus and* RICARDO *offscreen.*
ROSA (SINGING): . . . Alone with a heart meant for love . . .

Close-up—Ricardo
He looks up balefully and SINGS.
RICARDO (SINGING): . . . Alone.

Fade out

Fade in:
Interior, Ship's Corridor
DRIFTWOOD *enters. A* STEWARD *enters pushing a large trunk. He stops when* DRIFTWOOD *bumps into the trunk.*
DRIFTWOOD: Hey! Hey, that's mine. A trunk thief, eh? Where you going with that?
STEWARD: Suite Number Fifty-eight, sir.
DRIFTWOOD: Fifty-eight? That's me. Let's go.
DRIFTWOOD, HUMMING *"Pagliacci" climbs up on the trunk. The* STEWARD *pushes him forward. They bump into a trunk being pushed by a* SECOND STEWARD. DRIFTWOOD *slides off the trunk onto the floor.*
DRIFTWOOD: Hey, what's the idea? What's the idea? Hit-and-run driver, eh?
SECOND STEWARD: I—I'm sorry, sir.
DRIFTWOOD: Sorry, my eye. Look at that fender . . . it's all bumped out of shape. You'll pay for this, my good man. Let me see your number. Thirty-two, eh? Have you got any insurance?
SECOND STEWARD: What?
DRIFTWOOD: Are you insured?
SECOND STEWARD: No, sir.

DRIFTWOOD: Well, you're just the fellow I want to see. I have here an accident policy that'll absolutely protect you—no matter what happens. *(He pulls paper out of his pocket)* If you lose a leg, we'll help you look for it and all this will cost you is, uh, what have you got there? A dollar? *(He pulls a dollar out of the* STEWARD's *pocket)* One dollar. Here you are.

Close-up—Insert
The insurance contract. It reads:
HOTEL
MILANO
Sig. Otis P. Driftwood
Account due $540.00
PLEASE REMIT
Apparlamente

Medium Shot—Driftwood
DRIFTWOOD: All right. Let's go. *(*DRIFTWOOD *climbs back up on the trunk)* Suite Fifty-eight and don't go over twenty miles an hour. *(He hums* "Pagliacci" *again)*
The FIRST STEWARD *rolls the trunk away with* DRIFTWOOD *on top. The* SECOND STEWARD *stands in the corridor trying to figure out what happened.*

Full Shot—Three Bearded Aviators
They are standing in a line facing a STEWARD.

Medium Full Shot—the Same
They bow to the STEWARD *and turn together into their stateroom.* DRIFTWOOD *enters riding on the trunk, turns a corner in the corridor, looks over his shoulder at the* THREE BEARDED MEN.
DRIFTWOOD: Say, was that three fellows, or one fellow with three beards? *(As the trunk moves down the hall he looks into a room*

131

and sees GOTTLIEB'*s reflection in the mirror.* GOTTLIEB *is adjusting his collar and stroking his beard)* Hi, Gottlieb, always beating around the bush?

Medium Shot—the Ship's Corridor

As DRIFTWOOD *passes a closed door we hear crying behind it.* DRIFTWOOD *climbs down from his trunk.*

DRIFTWOOD *(to the* STEWARD *pushing the trunk)*: Wait a minute.

Interior, Rosa's Stateroom

DRIFTWOOD *enters;* ROSA *is lying across the bed.*

DRIFTWOOD: Anything I can do?

ROSA: Oh. Just a little homesick.

DRIFTWOOD: That's funny. I happen to have with me the greatest prescription for homesickness you ever saw. *(He takes a paper from his pocket)* A fellow gave it to me just before the boat sailed. There's the prescription and, uh, take it, uh, take it every two hours.

Close-up—Insert

A handwritten letter:

> Dearest
> I love you
> Ricardo

Two Shot—Rosa and Driftwood

She jumps up, hugs and embraces him.

ROSA: Oh!

DRIFTWOOD: I'm going out and get another prescription. *(He* SINGS *offscreen)* I yaa Pagliacci, I love you very muchee.

Interior, Mrs. Claypool's Suite

Door to hall is open as DRIFTWOOD'*s trunk chariot comes by. He dismounts and enters.*

DRIFTWOOD: Ah! Hello, Toots.

MRS. CLAYPOOL: Hello.

DRIFTWOOD: Hey, pretty classy layout you got here.

MRS. CLAYPOOL: Do you like it?

Medium Shot—Driftwood

DRIFTWOOD: Ah, twin beds. You little rascal, you!

Medium Shot—Mrs. Claypool

MRS. CLAYPOOL *(offended as usual)*: One of those is a day bed.

Two Shot—Driftwood and Mrs. Claypool

He sits down on bed and picks up a book from the table. She hurries to him.

DRIFTWOOD: A likely story. Have you read any good books lately?

MRS. CLAYPOOL: Mr. Driftwood . . . will you please get off the bed. What would people say?

DRIFTWOOD: They'd probably say you're a very lucky woman. Now, will you please shut up so I can continue my reading?

MRS. CLAYPOOL: No, I will not shut up. And will you kindly get up at once.

DRIFTWOOD *(rising)*: All right. I'll go.

Long Shot—Fuller Angle

DRIFTWOOD: I'll make you another proposition. Let's go in my room and talk the situation over.

MRS. CLAYPOOL: What situation?

DRIFTWOOD: Well, uh, what situations have you got?

MRS. CLAYPOOL: I most certainly will not go to your room.

DRIFTWOOD: Okay, then I'll stay here. *(He SINGS)* "Ridi Pagliacci tra-la-la-la." *(He LAUGHS, SINGS LOUDLY, walks to the open door and SINGS into the hall obviously trying to embarrass her)*

MRS. CLAYPOOL: All right. All right. I'll come, but get out.

DRIFTWOOD: Shall we say, uh, ten minutes? *(He looks at his watch and raises his eyebrows)*

MRS. CLAYPOOL: Yes, ten minutes, anything, but go!

DRIFTWOOD: Because if you're not there in ten minutes, I'll be back here in eleven—with squeaky shoes on.

He exits—MRS. CLAYPOOL *closes door.*

Interior, Ship's Corridor

DRIFTWOOD *dances,* HUMS, *and tips his hat as he walks down the corridor. Behind him the* STEWARD *pushes his trunk. When they get to his stateroom* DRIFTWOOD *opens the door.*

Interior, Driftwood's Stateroom

It looks suspiciously like a very small closet with a bed in it. DRIFTWOOD *enters and looks around.*

(See film still 7.)

DRIFTWOOD: Hey, wait a minute! Wait a minute! This can't be my room.

Medium Shot—Corridor

The STEWARD *shoves the trunk into the stateroom.* DRIFTWOOD *tosses his hat and coat on the trunk.*

STEWARD: Yes, sir. Suite Number Fifty-eight, sir.

DRIFTWOOD: Fifty-eight? That's an awful big number for a bird cage this size. Wouldn't it be simpler if you'd just put the stateroom in the trunk? Say, who was responsible for installing me in this telephone booth?

STEWARD: Mr. Gottlieb picked it out for you, sir.

DRIFTWOOD: Gottlieb, eh? Well, that's awfully decent of him, awfully decent. Did he pick out the whole room or just the porthole?

STEWARD: I'm sure you'll find it very cozy sir.

DRIFTWOOD: Cozy? Cozy is hardly the word for it.

STEWARD: Anything else, sir?

DRIFTWOOD: Yes. Tomorrow you can take the trunk out and I'll go in.

DRIFTWOOD *tries to enter the room past his trunk. He has*

134

difficulty shutting the door, and repeatedly pulls it toward him-self until he gets it closed.

Interior, Driftwood's Stateroom

DRIFTWOOD *moves around the trunk and onto the bed,* SINGING.
DRIFTWOOD (SINGING):

> Sing, ho! For the open highway
> Sing, ho! For the open . . .

Medium Shot—Driftwood

He stands on the bed, opens the trunk, as he SINGS. FIORELLO *and* RICARDO *stick their heads out of the trunk.*
(See film still 8.)

FIORELLO: Hello, boss. What are you doing here?

RICARDO: Hello.

DRIFTWOOD: Well, this makes it a perfect voyage. I'm terribly sorry but I—I thought this was my trunk.

FIORELLO: This is your trunk.

DRIFTWOOD: I don't remember packing you boys.

FIORELLO: You remember Ricardo Baroni—the greatest tenor in the world? You nearly sign him up once, you know.

DRIFTWOOD: Oh, sure. I just delivered a letter for you. How are you?

RICARDO: Pretty good, thanks. Just a little cramped.

DRIFTWOOD: Well, we're still in the harbor. As soon as we get out in the open ocean, there'll be plenty of room.

FIORELLO: Yeah, sure.

DRIFTWOOD: Say, isn't that my shirt you've got on?

FIORELLO: Hey, look out, I don't know. I found it in the trunk.

DRIFTWOOD: Well, then it couldn't be mine. Well, it's nice seeing you boys again but I was expecting my other suit. You didn't happen to see it, did you?

RICARDO *has gone around the back of the trunk and is occupy-ing himself trying to drink a glass of water.*

135

FIORELLO: Yeah. It took up too much room so we sold it.

DRIFTWOOD: Did you get anything for it?

FIORELLO: A dollar forty.

DRIFTWOOD: That's my suit all right. Say, it's lucky I left another shirt in this drawer.

Medium Close Shot—Driftwood

He leans over and opens the drawer. TOMASSO *is curled up in the drawer, sleeping.*

Three Shot—Driftwood, Fiorello, and Ricardo

DRIFTWOOD: That can't be my shirt. My shirt doesn't snore.

FIORELLO: Shhh. Don't wake him up. He's got insomnia . . . he's trying to sleep it off.

Close-up—Driftwood

He sits down on the bed.

DRIFTWOOD: That's as grizzly a looking object as I've ever seen. Well, get him up out of there.

Full Shot—All Four

They struggle to prop up the sleeping TOMASSO.

FIORELLO: He certainly is sleepy.

DRIFTWOOD: Well, I wish you fellows would explain this thing to me.

FIORELLO: Well, it's, uh, very simple. You see, Ricardo, he's in love with Rosa. Rosa, she go to New York. We want to go to New York, too, but we gotta no money, so we hide in the trunk.

DRIFTWOOD: Well, if you got no money, what are you going to do in New York?

RICARDO: Well, I can sing. There must be some place for me to work. Besides, I can be near Rosa, that's the main thing. Aw, you won't give us away, will you, Mr. Driftwood?

DRIFTWOOD: No, but you fellows have got to get out of here. I've

136

got a date with a lady in a few minutes and uh, you know the old saying, "two's company and five's a crowd."

FIORELLO: We go, but first we want something to eat. We no eat all day. We're hungry.

DRIFTWOOD: Well, we'll discuss the food situation later.

FIORELLO: We get food or we don't go.

DRIFTWOOD: I know I never should have met you fellows. All right, but you got to promise to scram out right after you've eaten.

FIORELLO: All right.

DRIFTWOOD: And I'll go and get the steward and you fellows be quiet. Remember, you're stowaways.

FIORELLO: All right. We no say nothin'.

DRIFTWOOD: All right. Now just, uh, just put that bag of jello over here, eh? Wouldn't it be simpler if you just had him stuffed?

They dump TOMASSO *on the bed.*

FIORELLO: He's no olive.

DRIFTWOOD: And I'll go and get the steward and . . . *(He turns and walks into the trunk)* Say, is this the door of the room or am I in the trunk?

FIORELLO: Oh. Over here.

DRIFTWOOD: Be quiet now. Don't make any noise.

FIORELLO: We no say nothin'.

DRIFTWOOD: I'll get the steward.

Medium Shot—the Corridor

DRIFTWOOD: Steward! Steward! Stew!

STEWARD *(offscreen)*: Yes, sir?

DRIFTWOOD: I say, Stew . . .

STEWARD *enters from around corner, left, rear.*

STEWARD: Yes, sir?

DRIFTWOOD: What have we got for dinner?

STEWARD: Anything you like, sir. You might have some tomato juice, orange juice, grape juice, pineapple juice . . .

DRIFTWOOD: Hey, turn off the juice before I get electrocuted. All right, let me have one of each. And two fried eggs, two poached eggs, two scrambled eggs . . .

Full Shot—Stateroom—Fiorello, Ricardo, and Tomasso
   TOMASSO *is on the cot asleep.* FIORELLO *listens at the door.*
DRIFTWOOD *(offscreen)*: . . . and two medium-boiled eggs.
FIORELLO: And two hard-boiled eggs.
DRIFTWOOD *(offscreen)*: And two hard-boiled eggs.
   TOMASSO *honks his horn from the bed.*

Two Shot—Driftwood and the Steward
DRIFTWOOD: Make that three hard-boiled eggs. And, uh, some roast beef—rare, medium, well done, and overdone.
FIORELLO *(offscreen)*: And two hard-boiled eggs.
DRIFTWOOD: And two hard-boiled eggs. *(Horn* SOUNDS *from inside the room)* Make that three hard-boiled eggs. And, uh, eight pieces of French pastry.

Full Shot—Stateroom—Fiorello, Ricardo, and Tomasso
   TOMASSO *is sprawled on the cot asleep.*
FIORELLO: And two-hard boiled eggs.
DRIFTWOOD *(offscreen)*: And two-hard boiled eggs. *(A* HONK *is heard)*

Medium Shot—the Corridor—Driftwood and the Steward
DRIFTWOOD: Make that three hard-boiled eggs. *(A* HONK *from inside room)* And one duck egg. Uh, have you got any stewed prunes?
STEWARD: Yes, sir.
DRIFTWOOD: Well, give them some black coffee. That'll sober them up.

Full Shot—Stateroom
FIORELLO: And two hard-boiled eggs.

Medium Shot—the Corridor—Driftwood and the Steward
DRIFTWOOD: And two-hard boiled eggs. (HONKING *in Morse code is heard)* It's either foggy out or make that twelve more hard-boiled eggs. And steward, rush that along, because the faster it comes, the faster this convention will be over.
STEWARD: Yes, sir.
DRIFTWOOD: Do they allow tipping on the boat?
STEWARD: Oh, yes, sir.
DRIFTWOOD: Have you got two fives?
STEWARD: Yes, sir.
DRIFTWOOD: Well, then you won't need the ten cents I was going to give you. (DRIFTWOOD *starts to the door)*

Two Shot—Driftwood and Fiorello
  DRIFTWOOD *comes back into the stateroom and* SLAMS *the door behind him.*
DRIFTWOOD: Well, that's fine. If that steward is deaf and dumb he'll never know you're in here.
FIORELLO: Oh, yeah, sure, that's all right.
  There's a KNOCK *at the door.*

Medium Shot—the Corridor—Two Maids
  They stand outside the door.
DRIFTWOOD *(opening the door)*: Yes?
MAID: We've come to make up your room.

Two Shot—Driftwood and Fiorello
  DRIFTWOOD *closes the door.* FIORELLO *stands in front of the trunk.*
FIORELLO: Are those my hard-boiled eggs?
DRIFTWOOD: I can't tell until they get in the room.

Full Shot—the Four of Them
  DRIFTWOOD *opens the door to let the* TWO MAIDS *in.*

DRIFTWOOD: Come on in, girls, and leave all hope behind. But you've got to work fast because you've got to get out in ten minutes.

FIORELLO: Hey, Tomasso!

RICARDO: Come on, Tomasso.

FIORELLO: Wake up. They goin' to fix the bed.

DRIFTWOOD: Say, uh, I'd like two pillows on that bed there, eh?

FIORELLO: All right, straighten up.

> RICARDO *and* FIORELLO *try to keep* TOMASSO *awake and off the bed as he falls over the* TWO MAIDS.
>> *(See film still 9.)*

DRIFTWOOD: Hey, there's a slight misunderstanding here. I said the girls had to work fast, not your friend.

FIORELLO: He's still asleep.

> TOMASSO *has the girl in a half nelson.*

DRIFTWOOD: You know, he does better asleep than I do awake.

FIORELLO: Yeah, he always sleeps that way. Now, he's half asleep.

DRIFTWOOD: Yes, he's half asleep and half nelson.

> *Another* KNOCK *at the door.*

FIORELLO: All right, come on.

DRIFTWOOD: Yes?

ENGINEER *(offscreen)*: I'm the engineer. I came *(he enters)* to turn off the heat.

> *The* WOMEN *are struggling with the bed;* FIORELLO *is struggling with* TOMASSO.

DRIFTWOOD: Well, you can start right in on him.

FIORELLO: Wake up, Tomasso. Tomasso, we're gonna eat soon.

DRIFTWOOD: You know if it wasn't for Gottlieb, I wouldn't have got this room. Just hold him there a second.

Medium Shot—the Corridor—Manicurist

> *She stands in front of the door holding her tray.*

DRIFTWOOD: Yes?

MANICURIST: Did you want a manicure?

DRIFTWOOD: No. Come on in.

140

Full Shot—the Crowded Stateroom—Driftwood, Fiorello, Tomasso, Ricardo, Engineer, and Two Maids

The MANICURIST *joins them.* DRIFTWOOD *reaches out to close the door.*

DRIFTWOOD: I hadn't planned on a manicure, but I think on a journey like this, you ought to have every convenience you can get.

Close-up—the Manicurist

She has her tray on her lap. TOMASSO *lifts his foot up into the scene and it lands on her tray.*

DRIFTWOOD *(offscreen)*: Hey, listen, I'm getting the manicure. Get out of here, will you?

Full Shot—the Crowded Stateroom

FIORELLO *struggles with the toppling* TOMASSO *as one* MAID *in foreground bends over bed. The* MANICURIST, *crushed against the door, works on the hand* DRIFTWOOD *offers her over her shoulder.*

MANICURIST: Did you want your nails long or short?

DRIFTWOOD: You'd better make'm short. It's getting kind of crowded in here. I don't know, this isn't the way I pictured an ocean voyage. I always visualized myself sitting in a steamer chair with a steward bringing me bouillon.

FIORELLO: Come on, Ricardo, put him up. *(He means the limp* TOMASSO*)*

DRIFTWOOD: You couldn't get any bouillon in here unless they brought it in through a keyhole.

Medium Shot—the Corridor

A HUGE WORKMAN *approaches and* KNOCKS *on the door with his hammer.* DRIFTWOOD *opens the door.*

HUGE WORKMAN: I'm the engineer's assistant.

Full Shot—the Crowded Stateroom

DRIFTWOOD: You know, I had a premonition you were going to show up.

141

The HUGE WORKMAN *squeezes past* DRIFTWOOD *into the room.*

Two Shot—Driftwood and the Huge Workman

DRIFTWOOD: Say, is it my imagination, or is it getting crowded in here?

DRIFTWOOD *pushes the* HUGE WORKMAN *out of the picture.*

FIORELLO *(offscreen)*: Oh, I got plenty of room.

KNOCK *at the door.*

DRIFTWOOD: Yes?

YOUNG GIRL *(entering)*: Is my Aunt Minnie in here?

DRIFTWOOD: Well, you can come in and prowl around if you want to. If she isn't in here, you can probably find somebody just as good.

YOUNG GIRL: Well, could I use your phone?

Full Shot—the Crowded Stateroom

TOMASSO *and the* HUGE WORKMAN *are pushed into an embrace.*

DRIFTWOOD: Use the phone? I'll lay you even money you can't get in the room.

FIORELLO: How do you do?

YOUNG GIRL: How do you do?

DRIFTWOOD: We're liable to be in New York before you can get to that phone.

Medium Shot—the Corridor—Charwoman

She KNOCKS *at the door and* DRIFTWOOD *opens it for her.*

CHARWOMAN: I came to mop up.

DRIFTWOOD: Just the woman I'm looking for. Come right ahead.

Full Shot—the Crowded Stateroom

DRIFTWOOD, MANICURIST, FIORELLO, *the* HUGE WORKMAN, ENGINEER, RICARDO, TOMASSO, MAIDS, *and the* YOUNG GIRL

142

are in the room. The CHARWOMAN *pushes her way in. The*
YOUNG GIRL *tries to use the phone.*
(See film still 10.)
YOUNG GIRL: Hello, operator?
DRIFTWOOD *(to* CHARWOMAN*)*: You'll have to start on the ceiling.
It's the only place that isn't being occupied.
FIORELLO: You can clean my shoes if you want to.
DRIFTWOOD *(to* YOUNG GIRL*)*: Tell Aunt Minnie to send up a
bigger room, too, will you?

Medium Shot—the Corridor
FOUR WAITERS *carrying trays approach the door.* FIRST
STEWARD KNOCKS *and* DRIFTWOOD *opens the door.*
STEWARD: Stewards.
DRIFTWOOD: Ah, come right ahead.

Full Shot—the Crowded Stateroom
FIORELLO: Hey Tomasso, the food!
The WAITERS *enter. (There are now* ELEVEN PEOPLE *in the
stateroom.)* TOMASSO, *still asleep, is thrown across a* WAITER'*s
tray.*
(See film still 11.)
YOUNG GIRL *(still on phone)*: Is my Aunt Minnie down there?
FIORELLO: Food!
DRIFTWOOD: We've been waiting all afternoon for you, steward.
YOUNG GIRL: I want my Aunt Minnie.

Medium Long Shot—the Corridor—Mrs. Claypool
She tiptoes along the corridor to the door and as she opens it
DRIFTWOOD, MANICURIST, STEWARDS, *et al., fall out and onto
the floor at her feet.*

Fade out

Fade in:
Exterior, the Ship at Sea—Night
There is a full moon.

Dissolve to:

Long Shot—First-class Ballroom

Some of the guests are dancing and others are seated at tables. Streamers float through the air.

Long Shot—Captain's Table

CAPTAIN: Ladies and gentlemen, it is with great pleasure . . .

Three Shot—Mrs. Claypool, Gottlieb, and Driftwood at Captain's Table

DRIFTWOOD leans behind MRS. CLAYPOOL and blows a paper tickler under GOTTLIEB's beard.

CAPTAIN (*offscreen*): . . . that I welcome you all on this, the final night of the voyage.

Another Angle—Captain's Table

The three bearded AVIATORS are seated on the CAPTAIN's left.

CAPTAIN: I cannot let the evening pass without paying a little tribute to our distinguished guests of honor, the three greatest aviators in the world.

The three greatest AVIATORS in the world stand and bow in unison, to a great deal of applause.

Two Shot—Driftwood and Rosa

DRIFTWOOD: The three greatest aviators but you notice they're traveling by boat.

Medium Shot—Captain's Table

CAPTAIN: We are honored by your presence, gentlemen. Thank you.

AVIATORS: Thank you. Thank you, captain. (*They bow in unison to the* CAPTAIN. *Music up*)

Long Shot—Ballroom

The GUESTS are dancing.

144

Three Shot—Mrs. Claypool, Driftwood, and Rosa

DRIFTWOOD *stands, leans over to a* WOMAN *across from him.*

DRIFTWOOD: Do you rumba?

WOMAN *(she rises, eagerly)*: Why, yes. Of course I do.

DRIFTWOOD: Well, take a rumba from one to ten.

Close-up—the Woman

Her face falls—she sits

Three Shot—Driftwood, Gottlieb, and Mrs. Claypool

(See film still 12.)

DRIFTWOOD'S *head is almost on the table. He wears a feathered party hat.*

MRS. CLAYPOOL: Mr. Claypool went to his reward three years ago.

GOTTLIEB: And left you all alone?

MRS. CLAYPOOL: All alone.

GOTTLIEB: With eight million dollars.

MRS. CLAYPOOL: Eight million dollars.

DRIFTWOOD: Listen, Gottlieb, you're just wasting your time. If Mrs. Claypool wants to marry a fortune hunter, she's always got me.

GOTTLIEB: Fortune hunter!

DRIFTWOOD: As a matter of fact, you can hardly call me a fortune hunter, because when I first proposed to Mrs. Claypool I thought she had only seven million. But the extra million has never interfered with my feelings for her.

CAMERA PANS RIGHT, *excluding* GOTTLIEB *from the scene.*

MRS. CLAYPOOL: If you had any real feeling for me, you'd stop associating with the kind of riffraff I've seen you going around with.

DRIFTWOOD: You mean Gottlieb?

MRS. CLAYPOOL *(as she talks,* DRIFTWOOD *wraps a streamer around a dinner roll)*: I mean those two uncouth men I saw you around the Opera House with. I'm very grateful they're not on board the boat.

DRIFTWOOD: Why—have they slipped off? *(He rises)*
MRS. CLAYPOOL: Sit down! *(She pulls him into his seat)*

Interior, Stateroom

> TOMASSO, FIORELLO, *and* RICARDO *climb out of the trunk.*
> TOMASSO *opens the door and looks into the hallway.*

FIORELLO: Hey, come on, we find something to eat.
RICARDO: Do you think it's safe? You know, if they catch us they'll deport us.
FIORELLO: What have we got to lose? If they deport us, they got to feed us. Come on, we take a chance.

> TOMASSO *leads the way with* TWO TOOTS *of his horn as they exit.*

Interior, Dining Room
Three Shot—Gottlieb, Mrs. Claypool, and Driftwood

> DRIFTWOOD *eavesdrops on their conversation.* CAMERA PANS RIGHT *as* DRIFTWOOD *turns to eavesdrop on the adjacent conversation between* LASSPARRI *and* ROSA.

LASSPARRI: Does it mean nothing to you that I'm the greatest singer in the world?
ROSA: But I love to hear you sing, Rudolfo.
LASSPARRI: Oh, no, no, no. Let me put it this way. I love you. I adore you. I would die for you. Now do you understand?
ROSA: I'm afraid I don't.
DRIFTWOOD: The whole thing is very simple. When he says he's the greatest singer in the world, that means he loves you. Personally, I don't believe either statement.
LASSPARRI: Oh . . .

> CAMERA MOVES IN FOR TWO SHOT—DRIFTWOOD *and* ROSA.

ROSA: There may be something in what you say.
DRIFTWOOD: I'll tell you something confidentially. The only tenor I could ever stand was a fellow of the name of, uh, Ricardo Baroni. Ever hear of him?

> *Music in background* PLAYS *"Alone."*

146

ROSA: Ricardo. I wonder where he is right now. Probably roaming over the countryside someplace. Ricardo always loved the open. He never could stand being cooped up.
DRIFTWOOD: He still doesn't like it.

Long Shot—Steerage Deck
Looking down onto the lower deck, the GYPSIES *in peasant costume are dancing.*

Medium Shot—Tomasso, Fiorello, and Ricardo
They sneak around the edge of the crowd and see a SHIP'S OFFICER *who smiles at them.*

Medium Shot—the Three of Them
The three walk forward through the crowd. A MOB OF GYPSIES *is singing "Santa Lucia" in the background.*

Medium Close—a Table
It's covered with huge platters of spaghetti.

Medium Shot—the Three of Them
They walk forward and stand next to a STEWARD *who hands a plate to a surprised* TOMASSO, *and then plops a great load of spaghetti on it.* TOMASSO *walks down the line in disbelief as they pile his plate higher with an artichoke, salami, bread, and cheese. The other two follow him down the line, and food is added to their plates.*
(See film still 13.)

Dissolve to:
Three Shot—Tomasso, Fiorello, and Ricardo
They are sitting on the stairs finishing their meals. TOMASSO *wipes his plate.*
FIORELLO: Well, Tomasso, you feela better now, eh? And you, Ricardo, how do you feel?

147

RICARDO: After a meal like that? Great. Why, I could sing my head off.

FIORELLO: Go ahead and sing.

RICARDO *(he rises and* SINGS*)*:

> Cosi, Cosa, it's a wonderful word,
> Tra la, tra, la

FIORELLO *and* TOMASSO *cross to a conveniently placed piano and harp.*

Medium Shot—Fat Musician

He's loading his plate at the food line. He sees TOMASSO *sitting at the harp.*

MUSICIAN: Hey, stop that! Get away from those instruments. *(He crosses to them)* What are you doing?

MEN: Please let them play.

CROWD *(ad libs)*: Let them play. Let them play.

MUSICIAN *(under* CROWD*'s protests)*: All right. It's all right with me. Let them play.

Long Shot—Steerage Deck

As the MUSIC *starts, people gather around* TOMASSO, FIORELLO, *and* RICARDO.

Medium Shot—Ricardo

CAMERA FOLLOWS HIM *as he walks through the* CROWD *and* SINGS *to the people.*

RICARDO *(starts to* SING*)*:

> There's an old Italian phrase
> It's an old Italian craze
> Every little bambina
> Says it the very first day
> Every sweet Signorina
> Says it the very same way
> These funny little words
> Don't really mean a thing
> It's just a phrase that nowadays

148

Italians love to sing.
Cosi cosa, it's a wonderful word
Tra la la la.
If anyone asks you how you are
It's proper to say cosi cosa
Cosi cosa—if a lady should ask you if you care
You don't have to start a love affair
Say cosi cosa.
Does it mean "Yes?"
Does it mean "No?"
Well, yes and no.
Cosi cosa—get together and sing, tra la la la.
It's easy this way so start today
And learn to say cosi cosa. Cosi cosa.

CROWD (SINGING): La la la la la la la la la la la. Cosi . . .

The people join in the SONG. *On long-held* NOTE, MAN *in background stuffs face with spaghetti.*

Long Shot—Steerage Deck

CROWD SINGING *and dancing.*

CROWD: . . . cosa, it's a wonderful word, tra la la la if anyone . . .

LONG PAN LEFT TO RIGHT *of* CROWD *and* DANCERS.

Medium Shot—Dancing Couple

CAMERA PANS *the deck as everyone begins dancing.*

CROWD (SINGING):

. . . asks you how you are
It's proper to say cosi cosa
Cosi cosa—if a lady should ask you if you care
You don't have to start a love affair
Say cosi cosa.
Does it mean "Yes"? No!
Does it mean "No!"
Well, yes and no.
Cosi cosa, get together and sing.

On the music that corresponds to the lyric "No" we CUT TO A
CLOSE-UP *of a* GIRL *mouthing "no" to a* MAN. *On word "Yes"
she says "Yes"—he kisses her cheek.*
CROWD:

> Tra la la la
> It's easy this way so start today
> And learn to say cosi cosa. Cosi cosa.

Long Shot—Steerage Deck
The GYPSIES SING *and dance, including* TOMASSO, FIORELLO,
and RICARDO.

Medium Shot—Women Dancers
PAN RIGHT *on line of* WOMEN *doing dance.*

Long Shot—the Crowd

Medium Shot—Women Dancers
Swirling high skirts; STRAIGHT ON SHOT.

Medium Shot—Gypsy Dancers
DANCERS *leaping.*

Long Shot—Steerage Deck
TOP SHOT *of whole deck.*

Medium Shot—Gypsy Dancers
Group dancing.

Long Shot—Gypsy Dancers
GROUP, *dancing.*

Long Shot—the Steerage Deck
SHOOTING DOWN *on* CROWD—DANCERS *have formed three
twirling circles with* RICARDO SINGING *in center.*

150

RICARDO (SINGS):

> It's easy this way so start today
> And learn to say cosi cosa. Cosi cosa.

Medium Close-up—Fiorello

He does a little run on the piano, ending up making a little-finger pistol at TWO GIRLS. *(See film still 14.)* CHILDREN *are gathered around the piano enjoying him. He "shoots" the last notes with his forefinger, stands, they* APPLAUD *and smile. He leaves right.* TOMASSO *enters from right. They* LAUGH *at him.* TOMASSO *mugs as he takes off his coat. He pulls out stool, spins seat up to his behind to the laughter of the children. He starts with a great cadenza, stops, looks at them, spits on his hands and rubs them together, and spins the stool down. He slams the lid of the piano on one hand. The hand goes limp and dangles. He swings it up and balances it on top of his arm and then slams his other hand. He begins painting the piano keys with his limp hand as if it were a brush. He "paints" the* CHILDREN'S *faces. They* LAUGH *and then he walks over and embraces a harp.*

Medium Close Shot—Tomasso

He's at the harp, rolls his eyes heavenward.

Medium Close Shot—Children Laughing

Close-up—Tomasso

He kisses the backs of his limp hands.

Medium Close Shot—Tomasso *(See film still 15.)*

He's at the harp. PEOPLE *in the background are seen through the strings of the harp. An* OLD LADY APPLAUDS *as* TOMASSO *starts to play "Alone."*

Medium Close Shot—People Listening

They're relaxed and enjoy the MUSIC.

151

Close Shot—an Old Man

He nods to the music; TOMASSO WHISTLES.

Close-up—Two Little Girls

They listen intently.

Close-up—Tomasso

TOMASSO *finishes "Alone."* PEOPLE APPLAUD; *he tweaks cheek of a* BOY *listening.*

Ship's Railing

LASSPARRI, *the ship's* CAPTAIN, MRS. CLAYPOOL, *and* GOTTLIEB *looking off right.*

Medium Shot—Tomasso

TOMASSO *rises, bows to* APPLAUSE, *then sees* LASSPARRI, CAPTAIN, MRS. CLAYPOOL, *and* GOTTLIEB.

Two Shot—Lassparri and Captain

They're at the rail, looking down on the steerage deck.
LASSPARRI: Those men, they can't be passengers on this boat. They must be stowaways.
CAPTAIN: Stowaways? Well, we'll soon find out. *(He leaves)*

Long Shot—the Steerage Deck—Ricardo, Tomasso, Fiorello in Center

TOMASSO *points out the* CAPTAIN.

Medium Close Shot—Captain and Officers

They hurry down the stairway.

Medium Close Shot—Tomasso, Fiorello, and Ricardo

They climb over the piano and the railing.

152

Medium Shot—Tomasso and Fiorello

They climb over the railing in the background.

Medium Close Shot—Officers

They are trying to push their way through the dancing CROWD, *chasing* TOMASSO, FIORELLO, *and* RICARDO.

Medium Shot—Tomasso, Fiorello, and Ricardo

CAMERA *shoots past the* CROWD *as* TOMASSO, FIORELLO, *and* RICARDO *climb down from the railing and are lost in the* CROWD. *The* OFFICERS *pursue them.*

Dissolve to:
Interior, Ship's Corridor

A tough looking SAILOR *stands guard. A sign behind him reads:*

DETENTION

CABIN

Over this the music is "If I Had the Wings of an Angel" played big.

Interior, Detention Cabin

Full Shot—Ricardo, Fiorello, and Tomasso

RICARDO *is asleep,* FIORELLO *paces, and* TOMASSO *stomps his feet and plays a "hyped up" version of "Cosi Cosa" on a comb.* FIORELLO *paces in rhythm to the song walking faster and faster until he grabs the comb from* TOMASSO *and throws it out a porthole.* TOMASSO *goes to the porthole and opens it to look for his comb. A torrent of water roars in and drenches them.*

FIORELLO: Oh, oh! Hey! You, you crazy . . . Why, you, you, crazy . . . you wanna . . .

TOMASSO *starts to crawl out through the porthole.*

153

Exterior, Ship's Porthole—Tomasso

He leans out of the porthole. A rope swings in from the left and TOMASSO *reaches for it.*
  (See film still 16.)

Another Porthole—Driftwood

He leans out and looks toward TOMASSO *and waves.*

Ship's Porthole—Tomasso

He leans out, looks over toward DRIFTWOOD, *smiles, and pantomimes a rope.*

Other Porthole—Driftwood

He leans out of the porthole and takes the rope.

Ship's Porthole—Tomasso

He gestures excitedly to DRIFTWOOD *to throw him the rope.*

Other Porthole—Driftwood

He flings the rope offscreen to TOMASSO.

Ship's Porthole—Tomasso

He catches the rope as it swings toward him. He waves.

Full Shot—Detention Cabin—Ricardo and Fiorello

They are yanking TOMASSO'S *legs as he hangs out of the porthole. They yank him back into the drenched detention cabin.*
FIORELLO: Good! You got it. *(He means the rope)* Fine. Now you go first and see if it's safe. Come on. Come on. Come on. Out you go.
  TOMASSO *turns and tries to run.* RICARDO *holds him;* TOMASSO *runs and splashes in place on the wet floor. They grab him and shove him out the porthole.*

154

Medium Close-up—Tomasso

He crawls through the porthole clinging to the rope.

Long Shot—Exterior, Ship and Ocean—Tomasso

TOMASSO *clings to the rope and splashes into the water.*

Medium Shot—Tomasso in the Water

He comes up and spouts like a dolphin.

Exterior, Porthole—Driftwood

He leans out.

Medium Shot—Tomasso

He begins to climb out of the water and up the rope.

Two Shot—Exterior, Porthole—Ricardo and Fiorello

They look out the porthole, cheering TOMASSO *on.*

Medium Long Shot—Tomasso and Driftwood

TOMASSO *climbs the rope,* DRIFTWOOD *leans out of his porthole and tries to grab the rope.*
DRIFTWOOD: You're all right, but the boat's too far away.

Medium Close-up—a Sailor on Deck

He's tending to TOMASSO'S *rope's pulley. He oils the mechanism. The rope begins to uncoil.*

Full Shot—Side of Ship—Tomasso and Driftwood

The rope begins to fall rapidly down into the water and TOMASSO *drops out of frame.*

High Angle—Tomasso

He drops toward the ocean.

Medium Shot—Tomasso

He hits the water with a splash.

Medium Close Shot—Exterior, Porthole—Ricardo and Fiorello

They look out at TOMASSO *from their porthole.*

Other Porthole—Driftwood

He leans out of his porthole looking down at the water.

Medium Shot—Tomasso

He thrashes about in the water.

Medium Close Shot—the Sailor

He oils the rope's pulleys and begins to crank it in.

Medium Close Shot—Tomasso

He holds onto the rope as he is pulled out of the water.

Long Shot—Tomasso

He holds on to the rope and is pulled alongside the ship.

Medium Shot—Driftwood

He leans out of the porthole. TOMASSO *is pulled up rapidly past him and out of the scene.*

Long Shot—Tomasso

He clings to the rope as it zooms up toward the ship's highest mast.

Medium Shot—Tomasso

He hangs from the rope high in the air at the top of the mast.

Interior, Detention Cabin—Ricardo and Fiorello

RICARDO *holds* FIORELLO, *who leans out the porthole.*

RICARDO: What's he doing now?

FIORELLO (*looking up at* TOMASSO): I think he's hanged himself.

Medium Shot—Tomasso

He's still at the high mast clinging to the rope; he begins to slide downward.

Long Shot—Tomasso

He slides down the rope.

Exterior, Porthole—Driftwood

He leans out his porthole and looks up at TOMASSO.

Medium Shot—Tomasso

He swings on the rope over to the side of the ship and starts to crawl in through a cabin porthole.

Interior, Aviators' Stateroom

The THREE AVIATORS *lie sleeping in the same bed, with their beards outside the covers.* TOMASSO *climbs through the porthole into their cabin.*
    (See film still 17.)

Close-up—Tomasso

He sees the beards and can't resist.

Medium Close Shot—the Three Sleeping Aviators

The MUSIC *becomes a blissful pastorale.*

Close-up—Tomasso

He smiles, gets an idea, turns, reaches for scissors, and pushes up his sleeves, his eyes never leaving the beards.

Full Shot—Aviators' Stateroom

Snapping the scissors, TOMASSO *walks stealthily to the sleeping* AVIATORS. *He lifts the first beard, and a butterfly (animated) flies out.* TOMASSO *goes after it with the scissors. As the butterfly flies away,* TOMASSO *turns back to the beards.*

Fade out

157

Fade in:
Exterior, New York Dock
A banner is seen:

WELCOME

TO THE

HEROES OF THE AIR

Dissolve to:
Long Shot—Ship Docking
In the foreground the BAND *is* PLAYING.

Dissolve to:
Another Angle—Ship Docking
A CROWD SHOUTS *greetings to the boat as it docks.*

Medium Close Shot—Dignitaries
Several DIGNITARIES *in top hats board the ship.*
CAPTAIN: How do you do? Gentlemen, it gives me great pleasure
to . . . *(*DRIFTWOOD *barges in)*
DRIFTWOOD: Quiet! Gentlemen, our distinguished guests have
asked me to represent them and to act as their interpreter. Now,
if you'll all follow me, I'll take you to their cabin and if they're
still in it, very few of us will come out alive. *(They all exit)*

Dissolve to:
Ship's Corridor—Driftwood, Captain, and Dignitaries
They approach the AVIATORS' *stateroom.* DRIFTWOOD KNOCKS,
opens the door and looks in.

Interior, Aviators' Stateroom—the Three Aviators
They lie bound and gagged, their beards cut off.

Corridor—Driftwood and Group
DRIFTWOOD: Pardon me. Our distinguished guests are having their
shredded wheat. They'll be right out.

The stateroom door opens and three suspicious looking versions of the aviators in ill-fitting uniforms and fake beards emerge. They are, of course, TOMASSO, FIORELLO, *and* RICARDO.

FIRST DIGNITARY: Gentlemen . . .

Medium Close Shot—Driftwood, Tomasso, Fiorello, and Ricardo
TOMASSO *salutes with his left hand, pulling out a few strands of his beard as he does so.*

FIRST DIGNITARY: . . . kind friends . . .

DRIFTWOOD *(snatches paper from* DIGNITARY*)*: Here, give me that. Let's cut this short. The whole thing is very simple. *(He rips paper)* They want you to go to the City Hall and the Mayor is going to make another speech. We can tear up the Mayor's speech when we get there.

Dissolve to:
Exterior, City Hall Steps

Long Shot—Driftwood and the Three Aviators, the Dignitaries, the Mayor of New York and Two Rows of New York's Finest
(See film still 18.)

MAYOR: And so, my friends, as Mayor of this great city, I take pleasure in inviting our distinguished visitors to tell us something about their achievements.

Two Shot—Mayor and Fiorello
FIORELLO: What'll I say?

PAN LEFT *to include* DRIFTWOOD *as he lights his cigar.*

DRIFTWOOD: Tell 'em you're not here.

FIORELLO: Suppose they don't believe me?

DRIFTWOOD: They'll believe you when you start talking.

FIORELLO: Friends . . .

CAMERA PANS *to include* DRIFTWOOD. FIORELLO *drinks a glass of water and wipes his mouth with his beard.*

159

Medium Close-up—Driftwood

We see some DIGNITARIES *in the background.*

DRIFTWOOD: Talk fast. I see a man in the crowd with a rope.

Close-up—Fiorello

FIORELLO *speaks into the microphone.*

FIORELLO: How we happen to come to America is a great story, but I no tell that.

Medium Shot—Driftwood and Fiorello

DRIFTWOOD *tries to leave, sees he can't, and stays against his better judgment.*

FIORELLO: When we first started out, we gotta no idea you give us this grand reception. We don't deserve it. And when I say we don't deserve it, believe me I know what I'm a-talkin' about. Eh?

DRIFTWOOD: That's a novelty.

FIORELLO: So now I tell you how we fly to America.

Close-up—Fiorello

FIORELLO *(into microphone)*: The first time-a we starta, we getta half way across when we run out of gasoline and we gotta go back. Then I take-a twice as mucha gasoline. This time we were just about to land, maybe three feet, when what do you think? We run out of gasoline again. Then we go back again and getta more gas. This time I take-a plenty gas.

The CROWD *in the background begins to look suspicious.*

Close-up—Henderson

HENDERSON, *a hard-boiled detective, and other* OFFICERS *look suspiciously at* FIORELLO.

FIORELLO *(offscreen)*: Wella we getta half way over . . .

Close-up—Fiorello

FIORELLO *(into microphone)*: . . . when what do you thinka happen? We forgotta the airplane. So we gotta sit down and talk it over. Then I getta the great idea.

160

Medium Shot—Driftwood, Ricardo, Tomasso, Officers, and Fiorello

FIORELLO *(into microphone)*: We no take-a gasoline. We no take the airplane. We take-a steamship.

Medium Close Shot—the Dignitaries
They look at each other baffled and disgusted.
FIORELLO *(offscreen)*: And that, friends . . .

Close-up—Fiorello
FIORELLO: . . . is how we fly across the ocean.
CAMERA pulls back. DRIFTWOOD enters and shakes FIORELLO's hand.
DRIFTWOOD: I'm going out and arrange your bail.
The MAYOR steps up to the microphone.
MAYOR: This is the Mayor again.

Close-up—Mayor
MAYOR speaks into microphone. CAMERA PANS LEFT, revealing TOMASSO. MAYOR turns to TOMASSO, who shakes head no.
MAYOR: And now I take great pleasure in introducing another of our heroes, who will tell you something of his exploits. Of course . . .

Close-up—Driftwood
DRIFTWOOD: From now on, it's every man for himself.

Medium Shot—Mayor and Tomasso
MAYOR: I would suggest you make your speech a little more direct than your brother's.

Close-up—Driftwood
He leans over to TOMASSO.
DRIFTWOOD: What'll you give me to set fire to your beard?

161

Medium Shot—Tomasso in Center, Others in the Background

TOMASSO *pours a glass of water and drinks the entire glass through his beard. He pours another glass, and offers it to the* MAYOR, *who nods his refusal.* TOMASSO *drinks it and pours and drinks a third glass.*

DRIFTWOOD: Well, we're all right as long as the water supply holds out.

Close Shot—Henderson and the Officers

They stare at TOMASSO.

Medium Close-up—Mayor

He is about to explode as TOMASSO *drinks a fourth glass of water.*

MAYOR: Please, the radio. Your speech!

Close-up—Driftwood

DRIFTWOOD: You know, they may have to build a dam in front of him.

Close Shot—Tomasso

He takes another drink of water.

Close Shot—Henderson

He steps forward, on the verge of collaring TOMASSO.

Close Shot—Tomasso

His beard is falling off. He smiles, tries to stick it back on.

Close Shot—Mayor and Henderson

They exchange glances.

Close Shot—Tomasso

Water runs down his chin into his beard.

Medium Shot—Henderson

CAMERA PANS HIM *as he walks over to* DRIFTWOOD.

HENDERSON: Hey, I think these fellows are phonies. *(*TOMASSO *drinks from the pitcher)*

DRIFTWOOD: What's that you say?

HENDERSON: You heard me.

DRIFTWOOD, RICARDO, *and* FIORELLO *talk double talk and gesture wildly. The double talk is actually the soundtrack run backward. What they say is:* DRIFTWOOD: Did you hear what he said—he said you're frauds and imposters, and that you absolutely don't belong here at all. FIORELLO *and* RICARDO *exit left.* DRIFTWOOD *turns to* HENDERSON *and the* MAYOR.

DRIFTWOOD: Do you hear what they say? They say they've never been so insulted in their life, and they absolutely refuse to stay here.

MAYOR: No, no, please. He didn't mean it. Tell them he didn't mean it.

More double talk.

DRIFTWOOD *(to* MAYOR*)*: Of course, you know this means war.

MAYOR: Now see what you've done!

HENDERSON: I'm sorry. *(He really means it)* I'm awful sorry.

Close-up—Tomasso

He drinks water from the pitcher again. HENDERSON *enters.* TOMASSO *lowers pitcher showing his chin to be completely bare of whiskers.*

HENDERSON: I apologize, and I hope you're not offended.

Medium Close-up—Tomasso and Henderson

TOMASSO *kisses* HENDERSON, *leaving wisps of beard on his face.*

Long Shot—City Hall Steps

TOMASSO *ducks under the table, the* OFFICERS *and* CROWD *run after him.*

Dissolve to:
Close-up (Insert)

A photograph in a newspaper. The picture is of DRIFTWOOD, RICARDO, FIORELLO, *and* TOMASSO. *The caption reads:*

HERE ARE THE THREE STOWAWAYS
WHO FOOLED CITY HALL!

Interior, Hotel Room
Medium Shot—Driftwood

He's seated at the dining-room table, holding the newspaper. A napkin is tucked into his shirt. RICARDO *enters,* SINGING.

RICARDO *(sings)*: Oh, I'll still remember the happy . . .

DRIFTWOOD: What are you singing about? Read this. *(He shows him their picture in the newspaper)*

RICARDO: What are you going to do?

DRIFTWOOD: Do? The first thing I'm going to do is throw those two gorillas out of here. And that goes for you, too. I thought I got rid of those mugs when I sold my trunk.

Interior, Bedroom
Medium Long Shot—Tomasso and Fiorello

They are asleep on a cot; on another cot an alarm clock RINGS. TOMASSO *hits the clock with a mallet; it stops ringing.*

Medium Shot—Driftwood and Ricardo

DRIFTWOOD *at the table,* RICARDO *at his right.* DRIFTWOOD RINGS *a small bell and* CALLS *out.*

DRIFTWOOD: Kiddies! Come on. Everything is piping hot.

Medium Long Shot—Bedroom—Tomasso and Fiorello

FIORELLO *(jumps up, puts hat on)*: Breakfast! Breakfast!

Medium Shot—Dining Room—Driftwood and Ricardo

FIORELLO *(offscreen)*: Good morning.

RICARDO: Good morning.

FIORELLO *(entering)*: Oh, boy, I'm hungry.

DRIFTWOOD: Read that. That'll take away your appetite.

FIORELLO *picks up the paper and looks at it.*

FIORELLO: Naw, that only makes me hungrier.

DRIFTWOOD: Come on, you're going to be late for jail. *(*FIORELLO *begins to put food on his plate)* Well, those certainly went like hot cakes. You know, this isn't the way I anticipated my breakfast. Well, I'm certainly getting enough of you fellows.

TOMASSO *enters. He puts all the hot cakes on his plate, and then adds syrup, catchup, and mustard. He makes a sandwich with a cup between two hot cakes, and then offers it to* FIORELLO.

FIORELLO: I no like cupcakes.

DRIFTWOOD *(*TOMASSO *takes cigar from* DRIFTWOOD'*s mouth, puts it between the hot cakes)*: No. I know when I've had enough. Say, wait a minute, wait a minute! That was a two-bit cigar. I just . . . No, it's bad enough to have to smoke those things without eating them.

(See film still 19.)

TOMASSO *picks up top of sugar bowl, dips a hot cake in sugar and uses the top of the bowl for a mirror and the hot cake for a powder puff.* FIORELLO *and* DRIFTWOOD *laugh.*

FIORELLO: Get out. Glad I didn't bring my vest.

DRIFTWOOD: I forgot to tell you, he ate your vest last night for dessert.

FIORELLO: He's half goat.

DRIFTWOOD: Yes, and that's giving him all the best of it. *(He searches in his pockets)* Thought I had another cigar on me.

TOMASSO *picks up a hotcake, dips it in powdered sugar and powders his face with it.*

Close-up—Catchup Bottle

TOMASSO *puts his finger into the top of an open catchup bottle.*

Medium Close-up—Tomasso

He puts the catchup on his lips as though it were lipstick.
DRIFTWOOD *(offscreen)*: He's going to smell like a vegetable salad when he gets through with that.

Medium Shot—the Four of Them

TOMASSO *picks up a vinegar bottle and puts the stopper to his ears and neck as if it were perfume. He takes a rubber glove out of his pocket, blows it up, and pantomimes milking a cow.*
DRIFTWOOD: You know, I've been looking forward to this breakfast. I've been waiting all morning, and this is how it wound up. Well, I'll take a quart and a pint.
TOMASSO *milks the glove into a cup.*
FIORELLO: A little of that, anyway.

Close-up—Driftwood

DRIFTWOOD: Why don't you fellows be nice? Get out of here before I get arrested.

Medium Shot—the Four of Them

FIORELLO: Naw, I'd like to stay and see that.
There's a KNOCK *at the door.*
FIORELLO: What's that? *(Another* KNOCK, *louder)* If it's a policeman knock once more. *(Another* KNOCK*)* That's good enough for me.
FIORELLO, TOMASSO, *and* RICARDO *jump up;* DRIFTWOOD *points to the fire escape and they hurry out.*
DRIFTWOOD: Come in.
HENDERSON *enters.*
(See film still 20.)
DRIFTWOOD *(*SINGS *falsetto)*: When the moon comes over the mountain and the mountain comes over the moon . . . *(Henderson looks around suspiciously)* Yes?

166

HENDERSON: You remember me. I'm Henderson, plain-clothes man.

DRIFTWOOD: You look more like an old-clothes man to me.

Close-up—Henderson
HENDERSON: Nice place.

DRIFTWOOD (*offscreen*): Well, it's comfortable.

Two Shot—Henderson and Driftwood
HENDERSON: You live here all alone?

DRIFTWOOD: Yes. Just me and my memories. I'm practically a hermit.

HENDERSON: Oh, a hermit. I notice the table's set for four.

DRIFTWOOD: That's nothing. My alarm clock is set for eight. That doesn't prove a thing.

HENDERSON: A wise guy! Well, I'll just take a little look around.

Long Shot—Both Rooms
We can see both rooms and the wall dividing them. HENDERSON *goes into the bedroom and looks around. In the other room,* DRIFTWOOD *gestures to* RICARDO, FIORELLO, *and* TOMASSO *as they re-enter the living room from the fire escape.* HENDERSON CALLS. DRIFTWOOD *hurries into the bedroom.*

HENDERSON: Hey, you!

DRIFTWOOD: Coming. *(He enters the bedroom)*

Medium Shot—Henderson and Driftwood
HENDERSON: What's a hermit doing with four beds?

DRIFTWOOD: Well, you see the first three beds?

HENDERSON: Yes.

DRIFTWOOD: Last night I counted five thousand sheep in these three beds, so I had to have another bed to sleep in. You wouldn't want me to sleep with the sheep, would you?

HENDERSON: Ahhh!

HENDERSON *opens the bathroom door and looks in, doesn't*

167

see anything he wants, and turns back into the bedroom and looks under one of the cots. DRIFTWOOD *goes back to the other room.* CAMERA PANS *with him as he stops* FIORELLO, TOMASSO, *and* RICARDO.

FIORELLO: Henderson, huh?

DRIFTWOOD: Yeah go on outside.

DRIFTWOOD *hurries them out onto the fire escape and then closes the door.*

HENDERSON *re-enters from the bedroom and opens the door onto the fire escape.*

HENDERSON *(offscreen)*: Hey, you! *(He re-enters)* Who are you talking to?

DRIFTWOOD: I was talking to myself and there's nothing you can do about it. I've had three of the best doctors in the East.

HENDERSON: Well, I certainly heard somebody say something.

HENDERSON *crosses to the fire escape and looks out.*

DRIFTWOOD: Oh, it's sheer folly on your part.

HENDERSON: What's this?

DRIFTWOOD: Why, that's a fire escape, and that's a table and this is a room, and there's the door leading out and I wish you'd use it. (À la *Garbo*) I, I vant to be alone.

HENDERSON: You'll be alone when I throw you in jail.

Exterior, Fire Escape
Full Shot—Ricardo

He stands on a ledge, hiding from HENDERSON.

DRIFTWOOD *(offscreen)*: Isn't there a song like that, Henderson?

HENDERSON *walks out on the ledge.*

Medium Long Shot—Tomasso and Fiorello

They carry one of the cots from the bedroom into the living room.

DRIFTWOOD *(offscreen)*: Look out. He's coming around the other way. (HENDERSON *comes into the bedroom from the fire escape*) Get inside quick. He's going to catch you.

168

Medium Shot—Living Room—Tomasso, Fiorello, and Driftwood

TOMASSO *and* FIORELLO *run in with the cot.*

DRIFTWOOD: And believe me, it means a stretch at the Big House if he catches you in here. Don't let him catch you in here.

HENDERSON *(offscreen)*: Hey, you!

TOMASSO *goes to the table and picks up the hot cake. He and* FIORELLO *hurry to the fire escape.*

DRIFTWOOD: Coming! (CAMERA PANS *him into the bedroom)*

HENDERSON: What became of that fourth bed?

DRIFTWOOD: What are you referring to, Colonel?

HENDERSON: The last time I was in this room there were four beds here.

DRIFTWOOD: Please, I'm not interested in your private life, am I?

HENDERSON *goes into the living room and sees the cot.*

HENDERSON: Ohhh! Say! What's that bed doing here?

DRIFTWOOD: I don't see it doing anything.

HENDERSON: There's something funny going on around here. *(He goes to fire escape)*

DRIFTWOOD: Not around here, there isn't.

HENDERSON: But I'll get to the bottom of it.

Medium Long Shot—Bedroom—Fiorello and Tomasso

They've come in from the fire escape, carrying the second bed through the door leading to the living room.

DRIFTWOOD *(offscreen)*: The stairs right there. Look out. Look out. (*HENDERSON re-enters the bedroom from the fire escape)* Now be on your guard, will you.

HENDERSON: Hey, you!

Medium Long Shot—Living Room—Driftwood, Tomasso, and Fiorello

They are at the fire-escape door. CAMERA PANS DRIFTWOOD *as he runs back into the bedroom.*

DRIFTWOOD: Coming!

HENDERSON: Am I crazy or are there only two beds here?

DRIFTWOOD: Now, which question do you want me to answer first, Henderson?

CAMERA PANS HENDERSON *into the living room.*

HENDERSON: Ohhh! Ah! Say . . . (DRIFTWOOD *joins him in the living room*) How . . . how did these two beds get together?

DRIFTWOOD: Well, you know how these things are. They breed like rabbits.

Close-up—Henderson

He stands with his back to the door. The door swings open and TOMASSO *enters with another bed.* HENDERSON *pushes the bed aside as if it were a door, using* TOMASSO's *hand as a doorknob and goes back into the bedroom.*

HENDERSON: Let me tell you something, I'll solve this if I have to stay here all night.

(See film still 21.)

DRIFTWOOD: Let me tell you something, if you're going to stay here all night, you'll have to bring your own bed.

Medium Long Shot—Living Room

(See film still 22.)

TOMASSO *stands in the doorway and holds the bed.* DRIFTWOOD *stands in front of him speaking.* TOMASSO *moves around the bed so he is concealed from* HENDERSON, *who enters and bumps into the bed.* DRIFTWOOD *exits into the bedroom as* TOMASSO *runs onto the fire escape, letting the bed fall to the floor.*

HENDERSON *(offscreen)*: One bed!

DRIFTWOOD: One bed? What are you talking about?

Medium Long Shot—Bedroom

FIORELLO *and* DRIFTWOOD *move the last bed toward the fire escape.*

170

Medium Shot—Henderson

He goes from the living room into the bedroom.

HENDERSON: Now they're all gone! I know I'm crazy!

Medium Long Shot—Living Room—Tomasso, Driftwood, and Fiorello

FIORELLO *takes a sheet from the bed,* TOMASSO *picks up a table full of dishes, and they all exit into the bedroom.* HENDERSON *comes from the fire escape into the living room which now has all the beds and looks like the bedroom.*

HENDERSON: Ahhh!

Medium Shot—Bedroom (Which Now Looks Like the Living Room)

FIORELLO *drapes a sheet over himself and sits in a chair.* TOMASSO *puts a blanket around himself and sits on* FIORELLO's *lap.* DRIFTWOOD *puts on a false beard, sits, and reads the newspaper.* TOMASSO *rocks back and forth pretending to be knitting with silverware.* HENDERSON *enters in background, comes forward into the room, and sees what he takes to be a tranquil family at home.*

(See film still 23.)

HENDERSON: Oh, I beg your pardon. I must be in the wrong room.

Iris Fade out

Fade in:
Interior, Rosa's Room
Medium Shot—Rosa

She sits at a piano. She PLAYS *and* SINGS.

ROSA (SINGS): I'm not alone . . .

RICARDO *enters through window.*

RICARDO (SINGS): As long as I find you . . .

ROSA *gets up and goes to him as he jumps down from the window. They embrace.*

ROSA: Ricardo!

171

RICARDO: So you thought you could come to America without me, huh?

ROSA: Oh, you fool . . . you dear, dear fool.

RICARDO: Because I'm in love with you, you call me a fool. Well, there may be something in that.

Close Two Shot—Rosa and Ricardo

They embrace. CAMERA PANS LEFT *and* MOVES IN *with* ROSA *as she hurries across the room and shuts the window, and then* PANS RIGHT *as she hurries back to him. They embrace again.*

ROSA: But what are you doing here?

RICARDO: The easiest thing in the world . . . an open window . . . a detective, and here I am.

ROSA: Oh, Ricardo, you shouldn't have. They'll, they'll only send you back again, perhaps even put you in jail.

RICARDO: Oh, I don't care, darling, it's worth it.

ROSA: Suppose, suppose I go to Mr. Gottlieb. Maybe he'll intercede for you.

RICARDO: Gottlieb couldn't do anything; besides, Lassparri's got to him first.

ROSA: But there must be something we can do. *(*KNOCK *at door)* Who is it?

LASSPARRI *(offscreen)*: It is I—Rudolfo.

ROSA *(leads* RICARDO *to the bedroom and shuts him in)*: Uh, come in.

LASSPARRI *(enters from right)*: Do you mind my dropping down?

ROSA: No, no, of course not, only, ahh, I was just going to take a nap.

LASSPARRI: Rosa, why do you do this to me?

ROSA: Do what, Rudolfo?

LASSPARRI: Whenever I want to see you, you make some excuse. You will not dine with me; you will not ride with me; you won't even take a walk with me.

ROSA: But, Rudolfo, you, you know how busy I am . . . my debut in America.

172

LASSPARRI: Have you forgotten that it was I who brought about your debut in America.

ROSA: No, no I haven't forgotten.

LASSPARRI: Then why do you treat me this way? *(He embraces her)*

ROSA: Rudolfo, I must ask you to leave.

LASSPARRI: Oh, come now, my dear, be sensible.

RICARDO *(opens the door)*: If you ask me, I think she's being very sensible.

LASSPARRI: Baroni! Well, now I understand. You did not tell me you had a previous engagement.

RICARDO: Well, now you know.

LASSPARRI: And I apologize, and now, permit me to withdraw. In a boudoir, two are company, three a crowd.

RICARDO: And just what do you mean by that?

ROSA: Please, Ricardo!

LASSPARRI: Surely I have made my meaning clear.

    RICARDO *punches* LASSPARRI.

ROSA: Ricardo!

LASSPARRI: You have not heard the end of this.

ROSA: I'm sure I haven't.

LASSPARRI: You may be very sure.

Fade out

Fade in:
Interior, Backstage of Theater
Medium Long Shot—Driftwood and Doorman

    DRIFTWOOD *enters. The* DOORMAN *sits and watches him.*

DOORMAN: Good afternoon, Mr. Driftwood.

DRIFTWOOD: Good afternoon, Tim.

DOORMAN: Ready for the opening tonight?

    The CAMERA PANS *with* DRIFTWOOD *as he walks backstage, humming the "Anvil Chorus." He stops to talk to* THREE WORKMEN *who are loafing and playing cards.*

DRIFTWOOD: That's all right boys. I was young myself once.

WORKMEN *(ad lib)*: Thank you. Thank you very much.

173

CAMERA PANS *with him as he walks into the midst of a chorus rehearsal.*

MUSICIANS *(ad lib)*: Good day, Mr. Driftwood.

DRIFTWOOD: And how are all my songbirds?

MUSICIANS: Fine.

DRIFTWOOD: Splendid. Sing well tonight now. *(He* HUMS*)*

DRIFTWOOD *walks to the elevator.*

ELEVATOR OPERATOR: Waiting for you, Mr. Driftwood. Step right in.

DRIFTWOOD: Thank you, Otto. *(He continues to* HUM*)*

OTTO: Nice day today, isn't it?

DRIFTWOOD: Oh, it has its points.

Medium Close-up—Elevator Door

The door opens and DRIFTWOOD *steps out.*

OTTO: Here you are, sir.

DRIFTWOOD: Thank you, Otto.

OTTO: That's all right, Mr. Driftwood.

CAMERA PANS RIGHT *with* DRIFTWOOD *as he sees a* PAINTER *taking his name off his door.*

DRIFTWOOD: What's all this? Uh, what's going on here?

PAINTER: You mean what's coming off here.

DRIFTWOOD: You can't do that.

PAINTER: Want to bet?

DRIFTWOOD: But that's my office.

PAINTER: I'm taking orders from Mr. Gottlieb. Go see him about it.

DRIFTWOOD: I'll go see Mr. Gottlieb and I'll break you, my fine fellow. (CAMERA PANS *with him as he slouches angrily down the hall)* Go see Mr. Gottlieb! *(He bangs on* GOTTLIEB's *door)*

Interior, Gottlieb's Office

Medium Shot—Driftwood

He enters and the CAMERA PANS *with him as he barges into the room.* LASSPARRI *and* MRS. CLAYPOOL *are seated in the background,* GOTTLIEB *and* HENDERSON *are in front.*

DRIFTWOOD: What's the meaning of this? If you think that I'm going to . . . *(He sees* HENDERSON*)* uh, well, if you're, if you're busy I'll, I'll return later. *(He turns and starts to leave)*

GOTTLIEB: Just a minute, Mr. Driftwood. We have some news for you.

DRIFTWOOD: News—for me?

Two Shot—Henderson and Gottlieb
HENDERSON *standing at left;* GOTTLIEB *seated at right.*

GOTTLIEB: Mrs. Claypool has decided to dispense with your services . . . immediately.

Close-up—Driftwood
DRIFTWOOD: Dispense with my services? Why, she hasn't even had them.

Two Shot—Lassparri and Mrs. Claypool
MRS. CLAYPOOL: I've warned you, Mr. Driftwood, if you continued to associate with those men, everything would be over between us.

Two Shot—Henderson and Gottlieb
HENDERSON: And you've been associating with them.

Close-up—Driftwood
DRIFTWOOD: How do you know? You couldn't find them.

Long Shot—All Five of Them
MRS. CLAYPOOL: You've disgraced me and the entire opera company.

GOTTLIEB: So as Mrs. Claypool's new business manager, I must request you to get out . . .

Medium Close-up—Driftwood (Over Gottlieb's Shoulder)
GOTTLIEB: . . . and stay out!

175

DRIFTWOOD: Just a minute! Just a minute! You can't fire me without two week's salary. That's in Section 10-A of my contract.

Two Shot—Henderson and Gottlieb
GOTTLIEB: I find that you have overdrawn your salary for the next six months.

Long Shot—the Five of Them
DRIFTWOOD: Well, in that case I'll take one week's salary.
GOTTLIEB (*rises*): You'll take nothing. Get out.

Close-up—Driftwood
DRIFTWOOD: Well, if that's your best offer, I'll get out but I'm not making a nickel on it. And as for you, Mrs. Claypool, I withdraw my offer of marriage. (*He bows*)

Two Shot—Lassparri and Mrs. Claypool
They look away icily.

Close-up—Driftwood
DRIFTWOOD (*to* LASSPARRI): And that goes for you, too.

Two Shot—Lassparri and Mrs. Claypool
They look after him even more icily.

Interior, Corridor

Medium Shot—Driftwood
He comes out of the office.
DRIFTWOOD: The thanks I get for working my fingers to the bone. (CAMERA PANS *him past his old office toward the elevator*) All right, Otto.
OTTO: Just a minute. (*He pushes* DRIFTWOOD *out as he tries to enter the elevator*) This car is for officials. Take the stairs.
DRIFTWOOD: The stairs! Why that's four flights!

176

Long Shot—Staircase
SHOOTING DOWN *four flights of stairs.*
DRIFTWOOD *(offscreen)*: I can't walk all that distance.

Medium Shot—Driftwood and Otto
DRIFTWOOD *looks down the four flights.* OTTO *stands behind him.*
OTTO: All right, I'll help you! *(He kicks* DRIFTWOOD *in the seat of his pants)*

Traveling Shot—Driftwood Bouncing Down the Stairs

Exterior, Back Door of Theater

Medium Shot—Driftwood
He is thrown out of the stage door.

Dissolve to:
Exterior, Central Park

Medium Long Shot—Tomasso, Ricardo, Fiorello, and Driftwood
(See film still 24.)
They sit forlornly on a bench. TOMASSO *falls, then he pushes the others.* DRIFTWOOD *falls onto the grass.*
FIORELLO: Now, there's room.
DRIFTWOOD: Well, that's all I needed. I'm certainly glad I met you boys. First you get me kicked out of my job—then you get me thrown out of my hotel—and finally you push me off a park bench. Well, there's one consolation, nothing more can happen to me.
A partially seen COP *reaches his hand in right holding a club.*
COP *(offscreen)*: Hey, get off the grass.
CAMERA PANS UP *with* DRIFTWOOD *as he starts to drink from a water fountain but the water stops flowing as soon as he leans down to it.*

177

DRIFTWOOD: Well, I was wrong. People drink too much water anyhow. I'm certainly glad you boys came into my life. I had a good job and was about to marry a rich widow. Now, I can't even sit on the grass.

FIORELLO: I'd give you my seat but I'm sitting here.

DRIFTWOOD: Well, that's an offer. I tell you I'd like to think it over for a couple of days. Where can I find you?

FIORELLO: Don't worry. Wherever you are, you'll find us.

DRIFTWOOD: No, I'm sick of that. Let's meet somewhere else.

Medium Long Shot—the Four of Them

TOMASSO, RICARDO, *and* FIORELLO *sit on the bench.* DRIFT-WOOD *stands by the water fountain at right.* TOMASSO *whistles and runs out right.* RICARDO *and* FIORELLO *run after* TOMASSO

RICARDO: It's Rosa!

FIORELLO: Rosa!

DRIFTWOOD *(spreads out on the bench)*: Well, at least I can get my bench back.

Medium Close-up—Tomasso, Fiorello, Ricardo, and Rosa

THREE MEN *cluster around* ROSA.

ROSA: Don't feel so badly, Ricardo.

RICARDO: Well, I can't feel very cheerful about being such a hurdle to you.

FIORELLO: We all make-a things bad for you.

DRIFTWOOD: What's the matter?

FIORELLO: Hey . . . what do you think? Uh, Lassparri, he get Rosa fired.

DRIFTWOOD: Lassparri?

RICARDO: Yes, he won't let her sing tonight.

DRIFTWOOD: Well, what do you know about that? Well, we've still got all day to think of some plans and believe me the way I think, I think it's going to take all day.

Fade out

Fade in:

Exterior, Street in Front of Theater

Long Shot—the Marquee
It reads:

TONIGHT

RUDOLFO LASSPARRI IN *Il Trovatore*

Dissolve to:

Interior, Backstage

Medium Shot—Doorway
DOORMAN *standing by door. A* WORKMAN *enters right and then exits left.* GOTTLIEB *enters in the background and comes forward. The* DOORMAN *greets him, gives him his mail.*
GOTTLIEB: Good evening, Tim.
DOORMAN: Good evening, Mr. Gottlieb. Plenty for you tonight. *(He hands him a stack of telegrams)*
GOTTLIEB: Thank you. Thank you.
DOORMAN: You're welcome, sir.

Dissolve to:

Interior, Gottlieb's Office

Medium Shot—Gottlieb
He enters the darkened room, turns on the light, puts down his hat and cane, HUMS. CAMERA PANS *right past him to* RICARDO, TOMASSO, *and* FIORELLO. TOMASSO *is shaking a can with his right foot and pouring from a bottle into a glass with his left, while* FIORELLO *spritzes water into a snifter in* TOMASSO's *hand. It looks like a living Rube Goldberg drawing.*
GOTTLIEB *(offscreen)*: What does this mean?

Medium Long Shot—All Five of Them
GOTTLIEB *looks at the group around his desk.* DRIFTWOOD *stands.*

179

DRIFTWOOD: Ah, just the man I want to see. Gottlieb, these are the worst cigars I ever smoked. *(He throws his cigar on the table)*
FIORELLO: Yes, and your ice isn't cold enough, either.
GOTTLIEB: Get out of here, all of you. I shall send for the police.

Close-up—Driftwood
DRIFTWOOD: Just a minute, Gottlieb. I'll tell you what we came here for.
FIORELLO *(offscreen)*: Yeah, we make you a proposish.

Close-up—Gottlieb
GOTTLIEB: Oh. So you're willing to give yourselves up, are you?

Two Shot—Fiorello and Driftwood
FIORELLO: Yes, if you let Rosa sing.

Close Shot—Gottlieb
GOTTLIEB: Well, I'm managing director and Rosa does not sing. But the rest of your proposition, giving yourselves up, that rather appeals to me. *(GOTTLIEB walks to the phone, picks it up. CAMERA follows him and includes TOMASSO.)* Give me police headquarters. Sergeant Henderson, please.

> TOMASSO *picks up a box and throws it into the air. It lands on* GOTTLIEB's *head. He collapses.* RICARDO *puts* GOTTLIEB *into chair.*

Dissolve to:
Interior, Orchestra Rehearsal Room

Long Shot—Musicians
> *The* ORCHESTRA TUNES UP. FIORELLO *and* TOMASSO *sneak in from left as* CAMERA TRUCKS IN.

Close-up—Insert
> *Music sheets for* Il Trovatore
> TOMASSO *reaches his hand in left and inserts music sheets for "Take Me Out to the Ball Game."*

180

Dissolve to:
Interior, Opera House

Long Shot—the Audience and Orchestra
The AUDIENCE APPLAUDS.

Medium Shot—Mrs. Claypool's Box—Mrs. Claypool
She sits and looks at the AUDIENCE *through her lorgnette.*
DRIFTWOOD, *dressed in* GOTTLIEB'*s tuxedo, enters from behind the curtain.*
DRIFTWOOD: Hello, Toots.
MRS. CLAYPOOL: Well, what are you doing here? This is Mr. Gottlieb's box.
DRIFTWOOD: He couldn't come so he gave me his ticket and he couldn't get dressed so he gave me his clothes. *(He puts his top hat on the railing; as he takes off his coat, the hat falls off the railing)*

Medium Shot—a Corner of the Audience Near the Orchestra Pit
The top hat falls into the scene.
MRS. CLAYPOOL *(offscreen)*: What?

Long Shot—Driftwood and Mrs. Claypool
DRIFTWOOD: Hey! Hey! Hey, shorty! *(He shouts down to a* MAN *in audience below him. The* MAN *picks up the hat and hands it up to* DRIFTWOOD*)* Atta boy! Here, here, get yourself a stogie. *(He tips the* MAN*)*

Medium Shot—Driftwood and Mrs. Claypool
DRIFTWOOD: Well, who's ahead?

Interior, Gottlieb's Office

Medium Shot—Gottlieb
He bursts in, dressed in his underwear. He strides to his desk and picks up the phone.

181

(See film still 25.)
GOTTLIEB: Get me police headquarters.

Medium Shot—Mrs. Claypool's Box—Driftwood and Mrs. Claypool
They are seated in the box. The STAGE MANAGER *enters the box.*
STAGE MANAGER: Mrs. Claypool.
MRS. CLAYPOOL: Yes?
STAGE MANAGER: Have you seen Mr. Gottlieb?
MRS. CLAYPOOL: Why, no. Isn't he backstage?
STAGE MANAGER: He's disappeared. We can't find him anywhere.
DRIFTWOOD: You didn't look in the right place.
STAGE MANAGER: But the speech . . . he was to make a speech before the curtain went up.
MRS. CLAYPOOL: Oh, dear, what'll we do?
Lights go out and a spotlight lights up the box. DRIFTWOOD *rises.*
STAGE MANAGER: That's the cue. Now you'd better say something.
MRS. CLAYPOOL: But I've never made a speech in my life.
DRIFTWOOD: All right, I'll take care of it.
STAGE MANAGER: You?
DRIFTWOOD: Uh, ladies and gentlemen. I guess that takes in most of you.

Medium Long Shot—Other Boxes
The AUDIENCE *looks confused.*
DRIFTWOOD *(offscreen)*: This is the opening of a new opera season . . .

Medium Shot—Driftwood
DRIFTWOOD: . . . a season made possible by the generous checks of Mrs. Claypool. *(He gestures for her to rise and then sit down)* I am sure the familiar strains of Verdi's music will come

182

back to you tonight, and Mrs. Claypool's checks will probably come back in the morning.

Medium Shot—Audience
Confused, they ad lib among themselves.

Medium Close Shot—Driftwood, Mrs. Claypool, and Stage Manager
DRIFTWOOD: Tonight marks the American debut of Rudolfo Lassparri.

Medium Long Shot—Audience Applauding

Medium Close Shot—Driftwood, Mrs. Claypool, and Stage Manager
DRIFTWOOD: Signor Lassparri comes from a very famous family. His mother was a well-known bass singer, and his father was the first man to stuff spaghetti with bicarbonate of soda, thus causing and curing indigestion at the same time.

Medium Shot—Orchestra Pit
FIORELLO *climbs into the pit from the rear.* TOMASSO *follows.*

Medium Long Shot—Driftwood and Mrs. Claypool
DRIFTWOOD: And now, on with the opera! Let joy be unconfined. Let there be dancing in the streets, drinking in the saloons, and necking in the parlor. *(He gestures to right)* Play, Don.

Close Shot—Conductor
He looks up and reacts negatively. The MUSICIANS *are seen in background. The* AUDIENCE APPLAUDS. *The* CONDUCTOR *turns to his right and bows, turns to his left, taps his music stand with his baton, and holds up his arms.*

Medium Shot—Tomasso and Part of the Audience

TOMASSO TAPS *his music stand with a violin bow.*

Long Shot—Fiorello, Tomasso, Conductor, and Orchestra

FIORELLO TAPS *on his music stand and* SPEAKS. *The* CONDUCTOR TAPS *on his music stand again.*

FIORELLO: I'll take this side.

Medium Shot—Tomasso and Part of the Orchestra

He TAPS *the music stand, and then* TAPS *on the railing and smiles.*

Close Shot—Conductor

He's aggravated and TAPS *more firmly on his music stand.*

Medium Close-up—Driftwood and Mrs. Claypool

DRIFTWOOD: It's none of my business, but I think there's a brace of woodpeckers in the orchestra.

Medium Close Shot—Tomasso

He's part of the orchestra. He holds up a trombone and draws a bow across it, as if it were violin.

Close-up—Conductor

He shakes his head "No" at TOMASSO.

Medium Close Shot—Tomasso

He puts down the trombone and waves the bow back and forth.

Medium Long Shot—Tomasso and Orchestra

TOMASSO *rises slowly and, waving the bow, walks toward the* CONDUCTOR.

Medium Close Shot—Conductor

TOMASSO *waves his bow back and forth. The* CONDUCTOR *backs up as* TOMASSO *enters left. They fence with violin bows; the* ORCHESTRA *rises.*

Medium Shot—Tomasso and Conductor

They fence as FIORELLO *and* MEMBERS OF THE ORCHESTRA *watch.* TOMASSO *picks up a music stand and uses it as shield.*

Medium Shot—Driftwood and Mrs. Claypool

DRIFTWOOD: Don't give up, boys! The cavalry is coming!

Long Shot—Corridor—Gottlieb

He enters the box, wearing DRIFTWOOD's *clothes, including the string tie. The outfit is several sizes too small.*

Medium Shot—Mrs. Claypool's Box

DRIFTWOOD *and* MRS. CLAYPOOL *in box. As* GOTTLIEB *enters the box,* DRIFTWOOD *climbs up on the railing, and crawls into the adjacent box, startling the people seated there.*

GOTTLIEB: Ah ha!

MRS. CLAYPOOL: Mr. Gottlieb!

DRIFTWOOD: I'll see you later.

MRS. CLAYPOOL: What are you doing?

DRIFTWOOD: It's all right. It's just the Tarzan in me.

Long Shot—Side of the Theater, Favoring Driftwood

DRIFTWOOD *balances on the railing.* GOTTLIEB, MRS. CLAYPOOL, *and* OTHERS, *watch him.* DRIFTWOOD *gives the Tarzan yell but jumps only into the box at left.*

Medium Shot—Mrs. Claypool and Gottlieb

GOTTLIEB: That Schweinhund!

Long Shot—Orchestra

CONDUCTOR *and* ORCHESTRA PLAYING *opening bars of* Il Trovatore. TOMASSO *and* FIORELLO *are in* ORCHESTRA.

Medium Close—Tomasso and Orchestra

TOMASSO PLAYS *trombone in blaring discord.* TOMASSO *picks up a hat and puts it over the trombone.* CAMERA PANS UP *with him when the hat's owner stands and takes his hat back, and then sits down again, angrily.*

Long Shot—Conductor and Orchestra

The CONDUCTOR *leads the* ORCHESTRA *as they* PLAY. TOMASSO *and* FIORELLO *are still in the* ORCHESTRA.

Medium Close Shot—Gottlieb

He opens the curtains on stage, looks out at the ORCHESTRA, *and sees* TOMASSO *and* FIORELLO *and reacts furiously.*
    (See film still 26.)

Medium Close Shot—Tomasso and Orchestra

TOMASSO *chews gum, takes the sheet music from his coat, and then sticks the gum on the back of the music.*

Close-up—Insert—Sheet Music

TOMASSO'S *hands stick the sheet music on the back of a musician's head. The sheet music reads:* Il Trovatore.

Close-up—Gottlieb

He peers out from behind the curtains, sees the chaos in the orchestra pit and clasps his hand to his forehead.

Close-up—Conductor

He is leading the ORCHESTRA. *The* AUDIENCE *is in the background.*

186

Long Shot—Orchestra

Close-up—Sheet Music

TAKE ME OUT TO THE BALL GAME

WALTZ

Close Shot—Conductor
He is confused as his ORCHESTRA PLAYS *"Take Me Out to the Ball Game." The* AUDIENCE *in the background is also confused.*

Medium Close Shot—Tomasso
He is PLAYING *the trombone. He puts it down and takes a baseball and glove from his pocket and plays catch with* FIORELLO. *He tosses the ball over the* ORCHESTRA *as they try to* PLAY *"Take Me Out to the Ball Game."*

Medium Long Shot—Driftwood
He comes down the center aisle toward the ORCHESTRA *with a basket of peanuts.*
(See film still 27.)
DRIFTWOOD: Peanuts! Peanuts! Get your fresh roasted peanuts folks. *(He tosses bags of peanuts into the* AUDIENCE*)*

Close-up—Gottlieb
He looks out from behind the curtains. He reacts and gestures wildly.
DRIFTWOOD *(offscreen)*: Very nice and hot and cold.

Medium Close Shot—Fiorello
He winds up to throw the ball. The MUSICIANS *near him duck.*
DRIFTWOOD *(offscreen)*: Get your peanuts.

187

Medium Close Shot—Tomasso

CAMERA PANS RIGHT *as he takes a violin from a* MUSICIAN *and holds it up like a baseball bat.*

DRIFTWOOD *(offscreen)*: Here you are. Peanuts. Ah, peanuts?

Medium Long Shot—Orchestra

FIORELLO *pitches the ball to* TOMASSO, TOMASSO *hits it with violin.*

DRIFTWOOD *(offscreen)*: Peanuts.

Medium Shot—Tomasso

MUSICIANS *grab the violin away from* TOMASSO. CAMERA PANS RIGHT *as* TOMASSO *runs off.*

Medium Shot—the Orchestra

The MUSICIANS *attempt to grab* FIORELLO *as he starts to run.*

Interior, Backstage Passageway

Traveling Shot—Fiorello and Tomasso

They run through the passageway and down a flight of stairs. GOTTLIEB *enters.*

GOTTLIEB: Ah, there you are . . . *(*FIORELLO *points at* GOTTLIEB's *clothing and* LAUGHS*)* . . . you . . . you . . . What are you laughing at?

FIORELLO: Those clothes don't fit you.

GOTTLIEB: Why, you, you . . .

TOMASSO *reaches into the scene and hits* GOTTLIEB *on the head with a shoe and knocks him out.* FIORELLO *shoves* GOTTLIEB *into a closet.*

FIORELLO: Hey, you're gettin' to be a good shot, Tomasso. The opera starts! Now we really go to work. *(They run upstairs)*

Interior, Rosa's Dressing Room

Two Shot—Rosa and Ricardo

In the background we can HEAR *the first notes of the opera. She goes to the door and listens.*

188

ROSA: The curtain's up. They've started.

RICARDO (takes her in his arms): Now, don't worry.

Dissolve to:
Interior, Backstage

Long Shot—Stage Manager
He runs down the stairs toward GOTTLIEB, *who is* POUNDING
on the closet door.

GOTTLIEB (from inside the closet): Come and open the door here!
Let me out of here!

The STAGE MANAGER *opens the door.* GOTTLIEB *staggers out.*

STAGE MANAGER: Herr Gottlieb!

GOTTLIEB (furious): Where are they? Where did they go?

STAGE MANAGER: What?

GOTTLIEB: What, he asks me! (He exits)

Another Backstage Area—Two Stagehands
They are working. GOTTLIEB *and the* STAGE MANAGER *enter.*
We can HEAR *the opera from the stage.*

GOTTLIEB (over and above SINGING): Did a couple of men come
up here?

STAGEHAND: What?

GOTTLIEB: What! All I get is what!

Long Shot—Gypsy Camp Onstage
In the background we can hear the SINGING.

Medium Close Shot—Gottlieb
PEOPLE *are crowded in the wings.* GOTTLIEB *pushes his way
forward. The* SINGING *continues in the background.*

Medium Close-up—Gypsy Woman
GYPSY WOMAN (SINGING):

189

            . . . Lieta . . .
            . . . (Gay) . . .
            . . . in sembianza . . .
            . . . (in appearance) . . .

Medium Close-up—Driftwood

He's in MRS. CLAYPOOL's *box.*

DRIFTWOOD *(above the* SINGING, *wriggling his fingers, mocking the* GYPSY WOMAN*)*: Boogie, boogie, boogie!

(See film still 28.)

Long Shot—Audience and Boxes

They are stunned at DRIFTWOOD's *behavior.*

DRIFTWOOD *(above the* SINGING*)*: How would you like to feel the way she looks? *(He means the* GYPSY WOMAN*)*

Medium Shot—Gottlieb, Stage Manager and Others in the Wings

GOTTLIEB *(above the* SINGING*)*: That is Driftwood's voice! I want him put out of the opera house!

MEN: Yes, sir.

Medium Close-up—Gypsy Woman

GYPSY WOMAN *(*SINGING*)*:

            . . . gioia interno . . .
            . . . (joy around) . . .
            . . . Echeggiano . . .
            . . . (are echoed) . . .
            . . . Cinta di sgherri . . .
            . . . (surrounded by guards) . . .

Medium Close Shot—Tomasso and Fiorello

They are onstage in gypsy costumes. They have joined the CHORUS. TOMASSO *puffs up his cheeks and mimics the* GYPSY WOMAN.

(See film still 29.)

Close-up—Gottlieb

Still in the wings, he sees TOMASSO *and* FIORELLO *onstage and the first stages of apoplexy begin.*

Two Shot—Tomasso and Fiorello

TOMASSO *sees* GOTTLIEB, *and he alerts* FIORELLO.

Medium Shot—Gottlieb in the Wings

His anger grows.

Two Shot—Tomasso and Fiorello

TOMASSO *takes off his shoe and looks over at* GOTTLIEB.
FIORELLO: That's right. You go talk to him. (TOMASSO *crawls off in the general direction of* GOTTLIEB)

GYPSY WOMAN *(offscreen):*
. . . Sinistra splende sui . . .
(Sinister pleasure on)
. . . volti orribili . . .
(the horrible faces)

Medium Long Shot—Audience

The STAGE MANAGER *and his* ASSISTANT *enter, looking around.*
STAGE MANAGER: I know he's in the audience some place.

. . . La tetra fiamma . . .
(the flame rises)

Medium Shot—Doorman

HENDERSON *and a small platoon of* POLICEMEN *enter. The* DOORMAN *rises.*
HENDERSON: Where's Gottlieb?
DOORMAN: On the other side of the stage.
HENDERSON: Come on, boys.
HENDERSON, *followed by the* POLICEMEN, *marches off.*

GYPSY WOMAN *(offscreen):*
. . . Che s'alza al ciel . . .
(which rises toward heaven)

191

Medium Close-up—Gypsy Woman

GYPSY WOMAN *(completing her aria)*:

> . . . s'alza al ciel!
> (rises toward heaven.)

Medium Long Shot—Driftwood

He leans over the balustrade between MRS. CLAYPOOL's box and the adjacent box.

DRIFTWOOD *(to a WOMAN in the next box)*: What was that? High C or Vitamin D?

WOMAN: Oh, you . . .

Long Shot—Gypsy Camp Onstage

The GYPSIES are SINGING and dancing.

GYPSIES: Allerta (Arouse ye!)

Medium Close Shot—Fiorello and the Gypsies

They dance in a circle.

Medium Shot—Gottlieb

He's in the wings looking out on the stage furiously.

Medium Shot—Fiorello and the Gypsies

They are SINGING and dancing.

GYPSIES:
. . . Chi del gitano . . .
(Who of the gypsy boys.)

Long Shot—Gottlieb in the Wings

He picks up a frying pan. HENDERSON enters, looks at him.

I giorni abbella . . .
(cheers the day)

Medium Close Shot—Henderson

He sees GOTTLIEB from behind,

GYPSIES *(offscreen)*:

192

assumes he's DRIFTWOOD *(*GOTT-LIEB *is still wearing* DRIFTWOOD'S *clothes).*

Chi del gitano . . .
(who of the gypsy boys)

HENDERSON *(sees* GOTTLIEB'S *back still dressed as* DRIFTWOOD*)*: Drift-wood!

. . . I giorni . . .
(the day)

Medium Shot—Gottlieb in the Wings

He is looking out onstage. He raises the frying pan to hit FIO-RELLO *as he goes by.* GOTTLIEB *misses his opportunity.*

. . . abbella . . .
(cheers)

Medium Long Shot—Gottlieb and Henderson

GOTTLIEB *waits with his frying pan for another opportunity. Behind him,* HENDERSON *picks up a second frying pan and creeps up behind* GOTTLIEB. *As* GOTT-LIEB *raises his frying pan,* HEN-DERSON *bops him on the head with his. Simultaneously the* SHOT WIDENS *to include* TOMASSO, *who creeps up behind* HENDERSON *and bops him on the head with another frying pan.* HENDERSON *and* GOTTLIEB *both fall to the floor, out cold.* TOMASSO *steps over their bodies and runs back onstage.*

GYPSIES *(offscreen)*:
. . . Chi del gitano i giorni abbella?
(Who of the gypsy boys cheers the days?)

Medium Close-up—Fiorello Dancing with Two Gypsy Women

TOMASSO *enters from behind the curtains and dances with them.*

. . . Chi del gitano i giorni abbella?
(Who of the gypsy boys cheers the days?)

Medium Long Shot—Henderson and Gottlieb

They are lying on the floor. The STAGE MANAGER *enters.*

STAGE MANAGER: What's the matter? What happened here? Mr. Gottlieb. *(He calls to* THREE STAGE-HANDS*)* Here, give me a hand.

GYPSIES *(offscreen)*:
La Zingerella . . .
(The gypsy girl)

Long Shot—Gypsy Camp on Stage

Two ADAGIO DANCERS *enter through the chorus. The* GIRL *runs from the* MAN *as he cracks a whip behind her.*

GYPSIES:
. . . Vedi! le fosche . . .
(See the day)

Medium Long Shot—Girl and Man with the Whip

The GIRL *cowers as the* MAN *threatens to beat her. He grabs her and throws her to the center of the stage. He follows her cracking his whip viciously.* TO-MASSO, *shocked at the* WHIP MAN, *picks up another whip. As the* MAN *flings the* GIRL *through the air,* TOMASSO *cracks his whip at the* DANCERS *and hits himself.* TOMASSO, *holding his backside, runs across the stage in pain.*

. . . notturne spoglie de' cieli sveste, l'immensa volta . . .
(is breaking through the night)
Sembra una vedova che al fin si toglie . . .
(It seems like a widow is taking off)
I bruni panni ond' . . .
(her mourning clothes in which)

Medium Shot—Gottlieb, Stage Manager, and Others Backstage

GOTTLIEB, *still in* DRIFTWOOD's *clothes, has regained consciousness.*

GOTTLIEB: Where are those men? Did you catch them?

STAGE MANAGER: No, sir. I'm sorry. They're, they're still out there.
GOTTLIEB: Still out there! I have an idea. Get me two gypsy costumes at once. (*He takes off* DRIFTWOOD's *jacket*)

Medium Long Shot—Tomasso and Gypsies Onstage

The GIRL DANCER *whirls across the stage.* TOMASSO WHISTLES. *The* MALE DANCER *knocks* TOMASSO *down and pushes him aside.*

CHORUS:
Chi del gitano i giorni . . .
(Who of the gypsy boys—the days)

Medium Close Shot—Fiorello with Gypsies in the Background

FIORELLO *is beating the anvil with hammers, sparks fly.*
    (*See film still 30.*)

CHORUS:
. . . abbella . . .
(cheers)

Medium Shot—Adagio Dancers, Tomasso and the Chorus in the Background

The MALE DANCER *pulls the* GIRL's *long skirt off.* TOMASSO *pulls her underskirt off.*
    (*See film still 31.*)

Chi del gitano i . . .
(Who of the gypsy boys)

Medium Shot—Tomasso and Chorus

The MALE DANCER, *struggling to keep his dignity, pushes* TOMASSO *aside. The* GIRL *enters and the* MAN *lifts her into the air. In the background,* TOMASSO *is busy ripping the skirts off all the* OTHER WOMEN.

. . . giorni abbella . . .
(cheers the days)
Chi del gitano . . .
(Who of the gypsy boys)
i giorni abbella . . .
(cheers the days)

195

Medium Shot—Driftwood

He's standing in the AUDIENCE. DRIFTWOOD: Now we're getting somewhere.

He sees someone coming and runs out. The STAGE MANAGER *and his* ASSISTANT *run into the* AUDIENCE *following him.*

CHORUS *(offscreen)*:
Chi del gitano i giorni ab-bella . . .
(Who of the gypsy boys cheers the days)

Medium Shot—Tomasso and the Adagio Dancers

She's in the air. TOMASSO *goes toward her and tickles her bare stomach.*

(See film still 32.)

. . . La Zingarella . . .
(The gypsy girl)

Medium Close-up—Lassparri and Opera Officials, Backstage

POLICEMEN *are in the background.*
LASSPARRI: I will not sing unless they are put off there.
OPERA OFFICIAL: Yes, sir.

Medium Shot—Adagio Dancers

Her feet are on his neck and thigh. TOMASSO *sticks his head through the* GIRL's *legs and* WHISTLES *and waves. The* MAN *pushes him away.*

CHORUS:
. . . gitano i giorno . . .
(the gypsy boy the days)

Medium Close-up—Gottlieb and Henderson

They are dressed as gypsies. They begin creeping onstage. GOTT-LIEB *has mayhem in his eyes;* HENDERSON *looks baffled.* GOTT-LIEB's *costume fits him only*

. . . abbella . . .
(cheers)

slightly better than DRIFTWOOD's
suit did. They begin to move
through the chorus.
   (See film still 33.)

Medium Close Shot—the Male Adagio Dancer
He is holding the GIRL DANCER   CHORUS:
on his chest. TOMASSO strikes a   del gitano i . . .
match on the MALE DANCER's   (of the gypsy boys)
arm and lights a cigarette.

Medium Close Shot—Gottlieb and Henderson
They are moving across stage as   . . . giorni abbella
subtly as they can.   (cheers the days)
   Chi . . .
   (Who) `

Medium Close-up—Tomasso
Smiling, he sees GOTTLIEB and   . . . del . . .
HENDERSON.   (of)

Medium Close Shot—Gottlieb and Henderson
They are moving toward TO-   CHORUS:
MASSO.   . . . gitano i giorni . . .
   (the gypsy boys the days)

Close Shot—Tomasso
He sees GOTTLIEB and HENDER-   . . . abbella . . .
SON.   (cheers)

Medium Long Shot—Tomasso
He runs toward the wings.   Chi del gitano . . .
   (Who of the gypsy boys)

197

Medium Shot—Tomasso

About to enter the wings, he sees the POLICEMEN.

. . . i giorni abbella . . .
(cheers the days)

Medium Close Shot—Tomasso

He sees the POLICEMEN in the wings on one side. He looks over his shoulder and sees GOTTLIEB and HENDERSON coming at him from the other side.

La Zingarella . . .
(The gypsy girl)

Medium Long Shot—Tomasso

He does the only thing he can do: he climbs up the scenery.

Medium Shot—Policemen and Stagehands

They watch TOMASSO go up the scenery, and start to follow.

Medium Shot—Tomasso

He is partly up the scenery when he begins moving away from them. We can see the shadows of the POLICEMEN on the scenery behind him.

Medium Long Shot—Tomasso

He jumps through the air, grabs onto a sandbag and swings across the theater like Tarzan. He grabs a batch of fly ropes with his feet and swings back.

(See film still 34.)

LASSPARRI (offscreen):
Mal reggendo . . .
(I assaulted)

Medium Long Shot—High Angle—Gottlieb and Stagehands
GOTTLIEB *points up at* TOMASSO.

Medium Close Shot—Tomasso Entwined in the Ropes
He looks down and lets the sand-bag drop. As it drops, he, upside down, slides down with the ropes.

Long Shot—Lassparri Onstage
Behind him the backdrop that is attached to TOMASSO'*s sandbag flies up in the air.* LASSPARRI, *singing his heart out, turns to watch the scenery disappear behind him.*

LASSPARRI:
. . . all' . . . assalto
(I assaulted)

Medium Long Shot—Tomasso in the Ropes
He slides down the rope again. The POLICEMEN *and others stand, looking up.*

Medium Close Shot—Lassparri

LASSPARRI *(SINGING)*:
Il suolo avea, balenava il colpo in alto . . .
(The foe lay extended, brightly my blade was descending . . .)

Medium Long Shot—Tomasso
He climbs the ropes. A POLICE-MAN *climbs up a ladder after him.*

Long Shot—Lassparri Onstage
The backdrops begin going up and down.

Medium Close Shot—Audience

They react to the changing back-drops.

Medium Shot—Lassparri and the Gypsy Woman Onstage

A forest scene drops in behind them.

Long Shot—Tomasso

He swings forward on a rope.

LASSPARRI *(offstage)*:
Che trafiggerlo . . .
(Scorn I owed him)
. . . trafiggerlo dovea . . .
(for the hatred that he bore me)

Medium Long Shot—Woman and Lassparri Onstage

A railroad backdrop comes down behind them.

Quando arres- . . . .
(when a magic)

Long Shot—Tomasso

Still high in the fly loft he swings from rope to rope all the way across the theater to the catwalk which he grabs with his legs. PEOPLE *standing below watch; some* SCREAM *as he almost falls.*

. . . ta, quando arresta, un moto . . .
(Power stay'd my arm uplifted. Wrath and scorn had from my heart at that moment drifted)

Medium Close-up—Stage Manager and His Assistant Backstage

They run toward TOMASSO.

Long Shot—Tomasso on the Catwalk

He runs along the catwalk. TWO OPERA OFFICIALS *lunge for him*

200

*but he jumps off the catwalk
back into the ropes.*

Medium Long Shot—Gypsy Woman and Lassparri Onstage

TOMASSO, *swinging in the ropes,
causes a backdrop featuring a
fruit wagon and a sign that reads:*
> WE NEVER SLEEP
> TAXI SERVICE

to drop, this time in front of
LASSPARRI. *The* GYPSY WOMAN
is left alone onstage. LASSPARRI
*punches the backdrop from be-
hind.*

The backdrop lifts up.

LASSPARRI *(SINGING):*
Un grido-vi-i-i-en dal cielo,
mentre un grido . . .
(as of warning close beside
me)

Medium Close Shot—Mrs. Claypool in Her Box

*She is stunned and baffled at the
confusion onstage.*

Medium Long Shot—Lassparri and the Gypsy Woman Onstage

*Another backdrop is lowered be-
hind him. This one has a battleship on it. He sees the battleship
and stamps his foot petulantly as
he continues to sing.*

LASSPARRI *(offscreen):*
. . . vien dal ci-i . . .
(of warning close beside me)
. . . a-e-lo che mi dice . . .
(Thus they whispered)

Medium Close Shot—Gottlieb and Henderson

*Still in their gypsy costumes they
are in the wings looking onstage.*
GOTTLIEB *(above the* SINGING*):* A
battleship in *Il Trovatore*!

Long Shot—Tomasso

Still in the ropes, he swings out across the stage. A POLICEMAN *also on a rope swings after him.*

Medium Long Shot—Tomasso

He hangs upside down on the rope and swings onto the stage, sweeping past LASSPARRI *and grabbing his wig as he flies by.*

LASSPARRI *(offscreen)*:
No -O-o- . . .
. . . O-o-n feri-i-ir . . .
(and this feud)

Medium Close Shot—Gottlieb with Henderson in the Background

GOTTLIEB *is getting desperate to catch* TOMASSO.

Medium Long Shot—Tomasso

He swings across the stage on his rope.

Medium Close-up—Gottlieb

As TOMASSO *goes over his head, he drops* LASSPARRI'S *wig on* GOTTLIEB'S *head.*

LASSPARRI *(offscreen)*:
Di quella pira! l'orrendo foco . . .
(Tremble ye tyrants. I will chastise ye)

Long Shot—Tomasso

He swings from the catwalk across the stage and through the back of the scenery.

Tutte le fibre . . .
M'arse av- . . . vampò . . .
(My flaming beacon ye have upraised)

Medium Long Shot—Lassparri and the Gypsy Woman

LASSPARRI *and the* GYPSY WO-MAN *are* SINGING *as* TOMASSO

Empi, spegnetela, o ch 'io fra poco . . .

crashes through the scenery behind them.

(Yes, by that burning pile)

Long Shot—Tomasso

He twirls around a pipe from which the scenery is hung like an acrobat.
(See film still 35.)

. . . Col sangue
(My death)
. . . vostro la spegner-r-rò
(wrath defies ye)

Medium Close Shot—Tomasso

He is doing exercises on the scenery pipe.

Ero già figlio pri . . .
(Your blood I'll scatter)

Medium Long Shot—Lassparri and Gypsy Woman Onstage

LASSPARRI, still SINGING, gestures to the wings ordering GOTTLIEB to do something about TOMASSO.

LASSPARRI:

. . . i-io pri- . . . ma d'amarti
(where it blazed)
Non può frenar-
(She was my)

Long Shot—Tomasso

He straddles the scenery pipe. In the background POLICEMEN are climbing the ropes, coming after him.

mi il tuo . . .
(mother ere I adored thee)
. . . martir . . . madre infelice . . .
(I'll not desert her)

Medium Shot—Gottlieb, Henderson and the Others

They look up at the action.

. . . corro a salvar- . . .
(though my heart)
. . . ti O, te- . . .
(break—Farewell)

Medium Close Shot—Tomasso

He waves to them but reacts less confidently when he sees the POLICEMEN coming toward him.

. . . co almen-n-n-no
(beloved one)
Corro . . . a morir
(I who implored thee)
O, te co al meno corre . . .

203

(My wretched mother can-
not)
. . . a morir . . . O, te- . . .
co almeno
(forsake, my mother I cannot forsake)

Long Shot—Policemen

They move along the pipe toward
TOMASSO.

Medium Shot—Tomasso

He walks along the pipe.

Medium Long Shot—Policemen on the Catwalk

One of the POLICEMEN *swings forward on a rope.*

Medium Long Shot—Tomasso

He opens a door painted on a backdrop and blows a kiss off
screen.

Medium Shot—Same—the Other Side of the Door

TOMASSO *steps through the door and falls out of frame.*

Long Shot—Gypsy Woman and Lassparri Onstage

TOMASSO *falls down the backdrop, ripping it as he falls to*
stage.

Medium Long Shot—Tomasso

He falls onto the stage. GOTTLIEB, HENDERSON, *and the*
POLICEMEN *run toward him.*

Medium Close Shot—Gottlieb

He shakes his fists.

Medium Close-up—Henderson

He smiles and signals with a crooked finger for TOMASSO *to come to him.*

Medium Close-up—Tomasso

He signals back to HENDERSON.

Medium Close-up—Gottlieb

He walks toward the stage holding a section of scenery for camouflage.

Medium Close-up—Tomasso

He sees GOTTLIEB *coming.*

Medium Shot—Henderson

In the wings, on the other side of the stage he comes forward, also holding a section of scenery in front of him.

Close-up—Tomasso

He looks right, then left, sees they're coming at him from both sides, turns and runs straight up the scenery, which is still torn from his last entrance.

Long Shot—Gypsy Woman and Lassparri Onstage

TOMASSO *continues up the backdrop.*

Medium Shot—Gottlieb

He gives up on his scenery camouflage and turns to follow TOMASSO *from another direction. The* POLICEMEN *hurry after him.*

Medium Long Shot—Tomasso

He is balancing on the scenery pipe, LAUGHING.

205

Medium Shot—the Light Switchboard

Medium Long Shot—Tomasso
Standing on the pipe, he grabs what looks like a convenient trapeze and swings toward the switchboard.

Long Shot—Tomasso
He flies through the air on the trapeze toward the switchboard.

Medium Shot—Policemen and Stagehands
They run to the ladder to climb up after him.

Long Shot—Tomasso at the Switchboard
He pulls down the lever controlling the lights in the theater and the lights dim.

Long Shot—Lassparri and Gypsy Woman Onstage
The lights in the theater go out. LASSPARRI *stops singing and someone* SCREAMS.
VOICE: Don't you do . . .

Medium Close-up—the Light Switchboard
A flashlight beam is seen and then the lights in the theater go back on. The ELECTRICIAN *and a* POLICEMAN *are on the platform beside the switchboard.*

Medium Close Shot—Stage Manager
He runs to GOTTLIEB. *Others are seen hurrying through the scene.*
STAGE MANAGER: Herr Gottlieb! Lassparri's disappeared.
GOTTLIEB: What?

Medium Shot—Gypsy Woman Onstage
She's confused, trying to figure out what happened to LASSPARRI.

Medium Shot—Tomasso

In the wings, he pulls on a rope which hoists LASSPARRI *upward in a piece of scenery, a scenery box.*

Close-up—Conductor

He TAPS *his baton in a futile attempt to regain order.*

Medium Close Shot—Stage Manager and Gottlieb in the Wings

GOTTLIEB: But we haven't even a tenor!

ROSA and RICARDO, in street clothes, enter in the background.

ROSA: Mr. Gottlieb!

GOTTLIEB *(walks to them)*: You are Baroni!

RICARDO: That's who I am.

Three Shot—Rosa, Gottlieb, and Ricardo

GOTTLIEB: Get into a costume! Quick!

RICARDO: What?

GOTTLIEB: I want you to sing. Get ready.

ROSA: Ricardo!

RICARDO: But I have no reputation, Mr. Gottlieb.

GOTTLIEB: Eh?

RICARDO: Beside, I couldn't sing with a strange Leonora. You see, I've been rehearsing with Miss Castaldi.

GOTTLIEB: So that's it?

RICARDO: That's it exactly.

GOTTLIEB: All right! Get them two costumes at once! Quick!

ROSA and RICARDO embrace.

ROSA *and* RICARDO: Darling!

GOTTLIEB pulls them apart and pushes them off toward the dressing rooms.

GOTTLIEB: Please! Please, after the opera! Please! Go ahead! Get ready!

Dissolve to:

Long Shot—the Stage

CAMERA SHOOTS PAST the audience to ROSA who is on stage.

207

Rosa (sings): Sull'orrida torre
Chorus (sings offscreen): Miserere
Rosa (sings): Ahi per che la mor- . . .

Medium Shot—Rosa Onstage
Rosa (sings): . . . te
Chorus (sings offscreen): Miserere
Rosa (sings): Con ali di teneb- . . .

Medium Close Shot—Ricardo
He's behind prison bars, SINGING through the windows.
Rosa (sings offscreen): . . . bro
Chorus (sings offscreen): Miserere
Rosa (sings offscreen): Librando si va
Chorus (sings offscreen): Miser- . . .

Medium Shot—Rosa
She staggers back from heart pains and bad balance. She leans against a paper pillar.
Chorus (sings offscreen): . . . ere
Rosa (sings): Ahi forse dischiuse
Chorus (sings offscreen): Miserere
Rosa (sings):

> Gli fian queste porte
> Sol quando cadaver
> Già freddo sarà!
> Quan-n-n-do

Chorus (sings offscreen): Miser-r-ere, Miserere
Rosa (sings): Cadaver freddo so- . . .

Medium Close Shot—Ricardo
He looks through the bars at his beloved.
Rosa (sings offscreen): . . . ra—
Ricardo (sings): Sconto col sangue m-m-mio.

208

Medium Close Shot—Driftwood, Fiorello, and Lassparri

DRIFTWOOD *and* FIORELLO *are next to* LASSPARRI, *who is bound and gagged. They are all in the scenery box suspended in mid-air by a rope.* FIORELLO *speaks over* RICARDO'S SINGING.

FIORELLO: Hey, do you hear that? That's real singing!

Medium Close Shot—Tomasso

He hangs from a rope looking down onstage, happy that RICARDO *and* ROSA *are* SINGING.

RICARDO (SINGS *offscreen*): L'amor . . .

Medium Close Shot—Ricardo

He is behind barred windows.

RICARDO (SINGS):

> . . . che posi in te!
> Non ti scordar,
> Non ti scordar, di me!
> Leonora, addio!
> Leonora-a-a-a . . .

Medium Close Shot—Mrs. Claypool

She raises her opera glasses to her eyes and looks down at the stage.

RICARDO (SINGS *offscreen*): . . . a-a-a-ddi-i-io . . .

Medium Shot—Audience

They are watching and listening to RICARDO.

RICARDO (SINGS *offscreen*): . . . addi-i . . .

Medium Close-up—Rosa Onstage, Singing

RICARDO (SINGS *offscreen*): . . . i-i-o . . .

ROSA (SINGS): Di te, di te scordarmi!

RICARDO (SINGS):

209

Sconto col sangue mio
L'amor che posi in te . . .
ROSA *(SINGS)*: Di te, di te scordarmi . . .

Medium Shot—Gottlieb, Stage Manager, and Others
They listen and smile.
ROSA *(SINGS offscreen)*: . . . Di te scordarmi—
RICARDO *(SINGS offscreen)*: Non ti scordar . . .

Close-up—Mrs. Claypool
She beams.
ROSA *(SINGS offscreen)*: . . . di te scordarmi
RICARDO *(SINGS offscreen)*: Non ti scord- . . .

Medium Shot—Audience
They too are pleased by the SINGING.
RICARDO *(SINGS offscreen)*: . . . armi . . .

Medium Close Shot—People in Boxes
Everybody is pleased.
ROSA *(SINGS offscreen)*: . . . Sento marcar- . . .
RICARDO *(SINGS offscreen)*: . . . Addio . . .

Long Shot—the Stage
ROSA *is on stage* SINGING *to* RICARDO, *who is still behind bars.*
RICARDO *(SINGS)*: . . . Leonora, addio—
ROSA *(SINGS)*: . . . mi Sento marcarmi—
CHORUS *(SINGS offscreen)*: Miserere
RICARDO *(SINGS)*: Sconto col . . .

Medium Close-up—Rosa

ROSA *(SINGING)*	. . . di te, di te scordarmi
RICARDO *(SINGING)*	: . . . sangue mio, L'amor che
CHORUS *(SINGING)*	. . . Miserere . . .

210

Medium Shot—Ricardo

RICARDO *(SINGS to her)*: . . . posi in te
ROSA *(SINGS offscreen)*: Di te scordarmi—
CHORUS *(SINGS offscreen)*: Miserere
RICARDO *(SINGS)*: Non ti scordar . . .

Medium Shot—Rosa

ROSA *(SINGS)*
RICARDO *(SINGS offscreen)* } : Di te scordarmi, Sento marcarmi : Non ti scordar di me, Addio Leonora, ad-d-i

CHORUS *(SINGS offscreen)* } Miserere, miserere, miserere . . .

Long Shot—the Stage

RICARDO
ROSA } *(SINGING)*: . . . i-o, Leonora, addio! . . . i-i, di te scordarmi di te, di te scordarmi, di te!

CHORUS } Miserere, miserere, miserere, miserere!

Translation for the above duet:

On the horrid tower oh, it seems that death
With wings of darkness is going free
Mercy, Mercy, Mercy
Oh, perhaps it opens, they open the door for him
Only when the corpse will be cold when the corpse will be cold
Mercy, Mercy, Mercy
I pay with my blood the love I have in you
Don't forget, don't forget me,
Leonora, good-by, Leonora, good-by.
Forget you!
Mercy, Mercy, Mercy
I pay with my blood the love I have in you
Don't forget, don't forget me.
Forget you, forget you, forget you!
Good-by, Leonora, Good-by.

I pay with my blood the love I have in you
Don't forget, don't forget
Good-by, Leonora, Good-by, Leonora, good-by.
I feel faint. Forget, forget you!
Mercy, Mercy, Mercy
Forget you, forget you, forget you!
> *At the end of the duet, the* AUDIENCE CHEERS *and* APPLAUDS.

Medium Shot—Tomasso
> *He is hanging on a rope, cheering and serving as the counter-weight for the scenery box that holds* LASSPARRI, FIORELLO, *and* DRIFTWOOD. *He loses his grip and begins to fall.*

Medium Shot—the Scenery Box with Driftwood, Fiorello, and Lassparri
> *It begins to fall.*

Medium Shot—Ricardo, Rosa, Gottlieb, and Stage Manager in the Wings
> TOMASSO *falls into* GOTTLIEB'S *arms.*
GOTTLIEB: Uh! Why, you . . .

Medium Shot—the Scenery Box—Driftwood, Fiorello, and Lassparri
> *They crash to the floor and fall out groaning.*
HENDERSON: Huh! So!
FIORELLO: Is this the Opera House?

Medium Close Shot—Gottlieb and Stage Manager, Gypsy Woman and Tomasso Behind Them
> *They stare at* LASSPARRI, DRIFTWOOD, *and* FIORELLO.
GOTTLIEB: Arrest those men! *(*TOMASSO *watches.* GOTTLIEB *grabs him by the shoulders)* And this one, too.

Medium Close Shot—Policemen Rush to Arrest Driftwood and Fiorello

DRIFTWOOD: Well, it's about time.

LASSPARRI *pulls the gag from his mouth.*

GOTTLIEB: Lassparri! Where have you been?

LASSPARRI: Been? Do you know what they did to me?

Medium Close Shot—Audience

They are standing and APPLAUDING.

Medium Close Shot—Lassparri

The STAGE MANAGER *is behind him in the wings.*

LASSPARRI: Hmmm. I'll sing them an encore that they'll never forget. *(He clears his throat and strides toward the stage)*

Long Shot—Lassparri

He strides to center stage. The AUDIENCE *in the foreground begins to* BOO.

Medium Close Shot—Audience

It BOOS *louder.*

Medium Long Shot—Lassparri Onstage

Something is thrown at him. The AUDIENCE *continues to* BOO *off screen.*

Long Shot—Lassparri

He crosses the stage and exits into the wings.

Medium Close Shot—Gottlieb and Stage Manager in the Wings

LASSPARRI *enters.*

LASSPARRI: Never in my life have I received such treatment! *(Takes*

off his wig) They threw an apple at me! *(In the background the* AUDIENCE *continues to* BOO*)*
GOTTLIEB: Oh!

Medium Shot—Driftwood, Fiorello, and Tomasso
> HENDERSON *and the* POLICEMEN *are behind them, holding them.*

DRIFTWOOD *(to* LASSPARRI*)*: Well, watermelons are out of season! *(The* POLICEMEN *grab* DRIFTWOOD*)*
LASSPARRI: Oh! *(He storms out)*

Medium Close Shot—Audience
> *They stand,* APPLAUD *and* CHEER.

Medium Close Shot—Mrs. Claypool, Gottlieb, Rosa, and Ricardo in the Wings
GOTTLIEB: You, Baroni, get out there—quick!
RICARDO: Oh, no. I'm under arrest, Mr. Gottlieb.
GOTTLIEB: What's that?
RICARDO: Well, if they're arrested I ought to be, too . . . *(He walks to* DRIFTWOOD, FIORELLO, *and* TOMASSO *who are guarded by* HENDERSON *and his* MEN*)* . . . and I can't sing if I'm arrested.
GOTTLIEB: Oh, you . . . you! What do we do?
MRS. CLAYPOOL: We must have them. They'll save the entire season.
GOTTLIEB: Well, what is it you want?
RICARDO: Well, I . . .
DRIFTWOOD: Just a minute. Let me handle this.
GOTTLIEB: All right, only quick . . . quick! What do you want?
DRIFTWOOD: First, call off that police dog.
HENDERSON: Huh?
GOTTLIEB: All right, anything, anything!
HENDERSON: Just a minute! These men are in this country under false pretenses and I'm going to do my duty.

GOTTLIEB: I'll be responsible for them. Besides, they came over here with Mr. Driftwood, and Mr. Driftwood is an employee of the opera company.

HENDERSON: Since when?

DRIFTWOOD: Since Baroni started singing. And wait till I get a hold of the guy that runs that elevator!

GOTTLIEB: All right. Anything. Please go out and sing. Please.

FIORELLO: Wait a minute. Wait a minute. Before he sings you gotta sign a contract, and I get ten per cent. *(He pulls a contract out of his shirt)*

DRIFTWOOD: Yes, and I get ten per cent, too. *(He pulls a contract out of his jacket)*

In the background we hear ROSA SINGING.

Medium Close-up—Ricardo and Rosa Onstage

(See film still 36.)

ROSA *(SINGS)*: . . . scordarmi

RICARDO *(SINGS)*: Sconto col sanguo mio

ROSA *(SINGS)*: Di te, di te scordarmi

RICARDO *(SINGS)*: L'amor che possi in to

ROSA *(SINGS)*: Di te, di te scardarmi

RICARDO *(SINGS)*: Non ti scordar

ROSA *(SINGS)*: Sento marcarmi

RICARDO *(SINGS)*: Non ti scordar di me

They embrace.

Medium Close Shot—Driftwood, Fiorello, Gottlieb, and Tomasso

They study the contracts.

FIORELLO: Now, where were we?

DRIFTWOOD: The uh, the party of the tenth part should . . .

FIORELLO: No. No. *(They each rip their contracts)*

DRIFTWOOD: No? The party of the eleventh part . . .

FIORELLO: Naw, no. *(They rip again as* TOMASSO *tears* GOTT-

215

LIEB's *coat.* GOTTLIEB *turns to* TOMASSO; TOMASSO *rests his head blissfully against* GOTTLIEB's *shoulder)*

Long Shot—Stage
RICARDO *and* ROSA *are on stage,* SINGING *triumphantly.*

Fade out

Fade in:

The End

Fade out